WHEN DOWN IS UP

WHEN DOWN IS UP

✦

...Life with a Down Syndrome son.

Melba J. Wilkat

iUniverse, Inc.
New York Lincoln Shanghai

WHEN DOWN IS UP

...Life with a Down Syndrome son.

Copyright © 2005 by Melba J. Wilkat

iUniverse books may be ordered through booksellers or by contacting:

iUniverse
2021 Pine Lake Road, Suite 100
Lincoln, NE 68512
www.iuniverse.com
1-800-Authors (1-800-288-4677)

ISBN: 0-595-34228-0 (pbk)
ISBN: 0-595-67079-2 (cloth)

Printed in the United States of America

I would like to dedicate this to all parents who walk life's path

with a special child,

To my husband, Albert, who encouraged me and stood by my decisions

throughout the years,

To my three remaining children, Hibby, Tom and Judy,

who always freely gave their help and love

to their special brother,

And most importantly to John, my son, my inspiration, who lives on in

the precious memories he left with us.

Contents

PREFACE

This is the story of a young man who was diagnosed with having Down Syndrome at birth, and later in his life diagnosed with also having Cerebral Palsy.

It is the story of a young man who had a wonderful way of seeing the world, through eyes that saw only the good in people, through eyes that saw humor in life, and through eyes that saw and gave love to those who were wise enough to look for it in him.

He never wanted people to see him as different, even though he did realize to some extent that he was. He always wanted to be accepted as "one of the crowd." It was when people were talking about him saying, "John has Down Syndrome," that he would always correct them saying, "I'm not Down Syndrome. I'm UP SYNDROME." And "Up Syndrome" he was, in so very many ways.

From John you could learn that the world is a place of many different people. It is a world where sometimes things are not as they seem, a world where brother turns on brother, and a world where sometimes the smallest gesture can mean everything to another person.

John was a loving, giving, funny, joyful and, for the most part, happy person who was dealt a hand in life that most of us could never imagine. He made the very best of the situation, and John was truly an "UP SYNDROME" young man. It was living with John that inspired me to write the following poem:

THE SPECIAL ONES

Smiling and bouncing and bursting with joy.
That's what you see in a Mongoloid boy.
Happy and pretty and maybe a curl,
That's what you see in a Mongoloid girl.

Theirs is a world where there's no petty thoughts.
No scheming or planning to satisfy wants.
No slander or cunning and no phony ways.
Unselfish and giving to all our amaze.

This strange Utopia that we're speaking of
Is a gift these children received from above.
Just think what a pleasure our lives could be,
Had we eyes, like their eyes, thru which we could see.

Kindness, compassion and loves everyone.
Children so special and having such fun.
Who could deny them their happiness here,
Living and loving and having no fear?

—November 7, 1973

So when is Down up? It's when you see life through the eyes of…a boy named JOHN.

Four Generations
1st Eva Heim, 2nd M.S. Heim, 3rd Melba Heim Wilkat,
and 4th John Albert Wilkat and siblings, Judith Wilkat,
Hibby Wilkat and Tom Wilkat

SEPTEMBER 22, 1967—MARCH 9, 2004 That's the way it reads at the cemetery, the beginning and the end. Funny how we can write something as trivial as a date and it means so much. But it's the dash between the beginning and the end that really matters.

It is the DASH that has been my life with John for the past 36 years. It is the DASH that really counts, the dash that brought happiness and sorrow. September 22, 1967 and March 9, 2004, two of the most horrific days in my entire life, and while I thought at the time that September 22nd was so horrifying, little did I know that March 9th could make that day in September 1967 seem like a walk in the park.

I DIDN'T KNOW…

That I could feel such complete despair. That my life could seem so futile and I couldn't seem to find a real reason for going on. John had become the biggest part of my life, my existence, and it was for him that I planned even the smallest of things that affected our family and our lives. The day began with preparing his breakfast; cutting up his fruit and making something he could enjoy eating. It ended with putting his television on a timer to turn it off after we had attended to his toileting needs. It was the beginning and the ending and in between there was his swimming and his lunch and dinner and finding something to interest him as he whiled away the hours of each day in the swimming pool or in his bed. This was his day, this was my day…and it is no more!

So what am I to do?

I DIDN'T KNOW…

That I could feel so helpless. Nothing I could do or say would change what had happened on March 9, 2004. I have relived each moment of that Sunday night before, trying to make some sense of things, trying to understand the meaning of it all, trying to think of any little thing I could have done to change what happened. I feel so helpless and inadequate. How could I have stood by his side and not realized that he was dying, how could I? I feel so utterly helpless.

So what am I to do?

I DIDN'T KNOW…

That I could cry so many tears and not run out. I hardly ever cried before and now I just cannot seem to stop, as if the tears would wash away the hurt and pain that I feel without him. Perhaps they can fill the hole that is inside me, but I am afraid it will never be filled no matter how many tears I shed. I am told that this is part of grief but it doesn't help. Nothing can fill my hours, my days and my years ever again like he did.

So what am I to do?

I DIDN'T KNOW...

That I could be caught off guard by such small things. I think I am finally in control and then a certain smell, or a slight breeze against my cheek, or perhaps an ad for some drink that he loved, maybe something said or heard on the television, just the smallest things and my thoughts turn to John. And again, I find myself crying without control. Even when I try to bury my thoughts or turn them to something else, the least little thing floods my mind with memories of life with John.

So what am I to do?

I DIDN'T KNOW...

That sorrow and pain could hurt so very much. That my body could ache without actually being sick...that my head and heart could hurt with physical pain and nothing is actually wrong with me. Words are spoken and I do not hear them. I feel I am losing my mind, I cannot remember things that I should and I don't want to go out of the house or see people because they will tell me how better off he is now and I don't want to hear that. I know it is probably true but I don't want to hear it, because I am not better off, so maybe I am just being selfish. I just know that I really, really want him back with me, so that I can tell him how much I love him and I need him. My whole being aches, with no relief.

So what am I to do?

I DIDN'T KNOW...

That I would hear him calling to me in the darkness of night. That I could actually feel his presence around me...that each bite of food I take reminds me of him, each new day brings thoughts of him.... I just didn't know that anything could be like this.

So what am I to do?

xiv   WHEN DOWN IS UP

I DIDN'T KNOW...

That John's life was such an enormous part of my life and my being, that his every thought and action had at least a small impact on my own life and with his leaving a large part of my life left with him.

So what am I to do?

THERE IS NO ANSWER!!!

1

THE BEGINNING

September 22, 1967. Before that day in history, nothing in my life had actually been a real catastrophe. I was 33 years old, married with three children and we lived a comfortable life, never actually wanting for anything in the way of physical needs. Just the day before, everything was going really good for all of us. I was expecting my fourth child and I had a feeling it was a little boy, since I had carried two other boys before and one girl. I just seemed to know. On the morning of the 21st, I woke up to find that my water had broken which had never happened before, and was quite puzzled since there was no indication of labor pains. Getting the other children ready for school and calling the doctor was the start of it all I guess. Dr. Hamilton said I needed to go to the hospital so as soon as the children were taken to school, my husband, Al, and I left for the hospital, taking our time as there really didn't seem to be any hurry. I actually thought that they would check me out and probably send me home, but I was admitted. The day just dragged by with nothing of importance happening until around 6 P.M. when one of the nurses checked the heart beat. She hurried out of the room and the doctor came in saying I needed to turn onto my left side and they started a drip of medication in my arm. It seems that they were having trouble finding a heartbeat. Later, they started medication to start labor and then I went to sleep. About 3 A.M. I woke up with a jolt of labor pains and within a few minutes was in the delivery room having my baby. It was a little boy.

He was born at 3:20 A.M. Friday, September 22, 1967, weighing 6 lbs. 3 oz. I thought that everything was going smoothly except that they put me in a room in the gynecology section instead of the maternity section giving the reason that no rooms were available at that time and they were

1

waiting for check-outs. Little did I know that they were waiting for the doctor to return to the hospital as the nurse in maternity noticed a simian crease in his hands. This is one of the signs of Down Syndrome, also called Mongolism. Dr. Hamilton got back around noon and came in to tell me the news. He suggested that a Pediatrician to be called in for a second opinion. This we did. Dr. Eto did not get to the hospital until after dinner that day. He confirmed the diagnosis saying, "You've got a Mongoloid here. I am sure of that." I had to call my husband and tell him. It was one of the hardest things I have ever had to do. I felt that my whole world had just dropped out from under me. I was having hot flashes, then chills. It just wouldn't stop. I had no earthly idea what Down Syndrome was or what a "Mongoloid" was or what it meant and nurses and doctors trying to explain to me only made it worse. On top of all of that, we now had to decide if we wanted to take the baby home or put him in a home. Al said he would stand by whatever decision I made. To complicate matters, we had chosen the name James which was in honor of my cousin, who was a prisoner of war in Viet Nam, but that didn't seem right to name a child like this after someone. It seemed not to be an honor. So we had to think of another name but none came to mind. I would not see the baby until we had made decisions and decided his fate.

Al went to work and then came the next night saying he had thought about names all the while and had come up with the name, JOHN. He said, "You know John was Jesus best friend and we don't really have any-one close to us who might be offended by that," so that was the name we chose for him, using my husband's name as his middle name and he became John Albert Wilkat.

The third morning after having had little to no sleep the two nights before, I woke up early as if someone was awaking me and immediately I knew that we had to take John home with us. I had gone over and over all options for the past couple of days, not being able to either eat much or sleep, crying to almost convulsions and feeling like the whole world had been laid upon my body. Then I woke up on the third morning and all of a sudden I was so hungry and I felt as if a thousand pounds had been lifted from my shoulders. I remembered a bird show at Grant's Farm in St.

Louis that I had attended. The trainers had white cockatoos that they would toss to each other and the birds had been trained not to flap their wings in the air but to curl up in a ball. I was so fascinated with this; it was so totally against nature. If these trainers could teach birds to do this, surely there was something I could teach my own son. I also thought of my little Chihuahua dog at home that I dearly loved. I never expected that little dog to stand on two feet or talk, yet I loved her and she loved me…and she was a dog. My roommate remarked that I looked so happy when she saw me, and when the doctor came he said your face is just radiant. I told him of the decision I had made, to take John home and do the best I could, if only just to love him. Dr. Hamilton told me he had prayed I would make this decision and he was so happy. Dr. Eto, on the other hand, was not so kind. He told me I was making the worst mistake of my life, not only for me but also for my other children. I had three children at home, Hibby who was 13 years old, Tommy who was 8 years old and Judy who would be 6 years old her next birthday.

Dr. Eto said it would not be fair to them to have a child "like this" to compete with. He asked why I would choose this and I told him about the birds and about the little dog at home and I thought I could do something better than just getting rid of John by putting him in a home. He just shook his head and left the room. He never really understood.

The nurses had been waiting for this news and I had hardly gotten the words out of my mouth when they appeared with John. He wasn't the distorted, twisted, horrible sight I had imagined at all…he was a beautiful little baby, and he was mine. And so it was to be. We took John home and our journey began.

Neighbors and well-wishers came by with food, flowers, encouragement and love. Our house was filled with the blessings and good wishes of people we didn't even know were our friends. Our relatives came and on the first evening they were having dinner with us with all the wonderful food that had been provided by others. My mother had been on a trip to Canada when John was born and we had telegraphed her of his birth but it wasn't until she returned home that she learned about this tragedy that had taken over our family. She phoned me from her home in Little Rock and, when I answered the phone, I was laughing. My mother was horrified. Her first words to me were, "How can you laugh at a time like this when you have just had a child that's a Mongoloid?"

After getting over the hurt that I felt, my reply to her was, "Mom, you know I cried my heart out for three days and it didn't change a thing so I decided not to cry any more and just do the very best that I can." I cannot say that I never cried any more but I tried to do the best that I could and my family followed suit. My children always took up the shield when any mention was made of John that they did not approve of. They were like a mother bear with her cubs if anyone tried to put him down. They always came to his defense.

2

THEY TOOK UP THE SHIELD

You would expect a mother to be a guardian for her child. Even animals in the wild are protected by the mother. It isn't necessarily the case with siblings who could very well resent a new child especially one with special needs. Resentment many times manifests itself in older children when a new baby is brought into a home. This was not the case with John's brothers and sister.

The day I came home from the hospital with John I was very tired and trying to rest when all of a sudden I heard children's voices and looked up to see my daughter, Judy, with school friends she had brought home to see her new baby brother. She was so excited telling them all about him and how he "was different." It was almost as if she was proud of this. All the children "oooed and ahhhed" him and then they went home to tell their parents about Judy's brother.

Hibby was another one. Every day he would hurry home from school and first put John in a baby buggy and later, when John could sit, a stroller, and away they would go all over the neighborhood. Up and down the street and around the block. Hibby stopping as people came up to see the baby. You would have thought it was his child. It made no matter the weather, except for rain. He would bundle John up and away they would go. Sometimes John was finishing his nap when Hibby got home but he would wake him and their journey began. I had one neighbor say to me, "You shouldn't make Hibby take care of John every day when he gets home from school. He needs his own time." I told her, it was Hibby's choice and I probably couldn't stop him if I tried. He wanted to do this

5

and so he did it. Later, when we were rearranging the bedroom placement in our house, Hibby insisted that John share a room with him. I tried to point out that there were times when John needed to be sleeping and might disturb him but there was no reasoning with him, he insisted on John sharing his room, which he did until Hibby left for college.

In April of 1969, Tommy's class was asked by the teacher to write an essay. The theme of this essay was "If you had one wish, what would it be?" Following is the essay Tom wrote and the remark written by his teacher:

"One Little Wish

If I could have one wish, and I know it would come true, I would wish that my brother was like any other boy. My brother is mentally retarded and if I had one wish that's what I would wish for."

Teacher's reply:

"Dear Tommy,

This is a lovely wish. You are thinking of others instead of yourself. Sometimes we must learn to live with things as they are, and do whatever can be done to help those who are less fortunate."

Later, at a conference with his teacher, she told me that she just cried when she read his essay. She said that every other child in the class had wished for money or new clothes or new toys or things that were selfish wishes. She was worried that this was weighing heavily on Tom's mind and that he might need some kind of help. She didn't know Tom that well. He loved his brother probably more than he would have if he had been normal.

Judy was the one who really took up the shield. She was ready to fight anyone who had anything negative to say about John. When she was in a Science class in Junior High school they were studying mentality and genetics. One of the books told about Down Syndrome and said people with Down Syndrome had the mentality of Idiots.

Well, wave the RED flag. She went to the teacher and told her about John and that she was very upset about what was being told to the students. She asked if she could bring her brother to the class so they could see that the teachings in this particular book were not correct. I got a call from the teacher who knew nothing about Down Syndrome and needed my help in this endeavor. She asked if I would bring John to the class so the children could see him. At first I hesitated, as I didn't want to put John "on display." Then I thought, what better way to understand this than to see it first hand. We went to class and John walked around and talked to the kids and they loved him. He happily showed them the palms of his hands with the simian crease. I told them what I knew about Down Syndrome, not that it was a lot as I was still learning myself. I explained that there were three types of Downs. Trisomy 21, which was where the person has three of the 21st chromosomes instead of two, as in normal people. This is the one most people have and what John had. Then there was Translocation, which was when the 21st chromosome attached itself to other chromosomes. The persons with this type seemed to be more retarded mentally. And finally, there is Mosaic where only part of a person's cells is affected and depending on how many, this would determine the mental status of that person. One doctor told me that there are probably lots of folks walking around with this type and because it hadn't affected them too much they were "passing as normal." The class was more than interested and didn't want us to go. John had made a hit with all of them. Later, the teacher told me that she had been having trouble with three boys in the back of the room. They never paid attention and many times caused trouble. She said after we had been there, they wanted to learn more about mental retardation and insisted on writing a letter to the publisher of the book they had read and tell them that their information was wrong. The class did this and all the students signed the letter. John was doing some good already.

Later, after we moved to Florida, in another class, the teacher made a remark that retarded people should be placed in homes. Judy packed up her books and went to the counselor's office. I got another phone call as she was refusing to go back to class. We finally settled on, "O K, the teacher would apologize to Judy and take back what she had said about retarded people and she would correct the information she had given the class."

My son-in-law told me later, after they were married, he knew he had to like John if he wanted to make any impression on Judy or be any part of her life. He did like John and was a big part of John's life, always helping with his care and truly being a 'brother' to John. John called him "My professional help."

None of the three siblings ever neglected John and they always made sure he was included in any event that was happening. He was never an embarrassment to them nor were they ashamed of him, as Dr. Eto had told me when John was born. He didn't know my kids!!

3

THE INFANT YEARS

Right after I came home with John from the hospital, I received the following poem in the mail. I put it in a frame beside a picture of a little boy angel and that hung in John's room the rest of his life. Feeling it fitting, we removed it from the wall and placed it beside John in his coffin, to be with him forever. This is the poem:

> Oh, please…
> Turn not your head or hide me in the dark.
> Shed not a quiet tear or lower your eyes in shame.
> I am flesh and blood with heart and soul.
> I need your love and understanding, too.
> Accept me as He put me here…
> A child to love, No more, no less…

He would remain that, a child to love, no more, no less and we were never ashamed of him but rather pitied anyone who felt differently than we did. John was a wonderful person and, in his short time on this earth, he probably did more for other people than most of us achieve in a lifetime. His life affected more people than I ever knew. Even today, people are telling me how much John meant to them and how in some small way knowing him had changed their lives.

I started a journal about John almost immediately as I wanted to keep accurate information about his advances and achievements. With my other children I had not been as diligent as theirs had been normal births and childhoods. I also started writing poems about my feelings about John and his life. One of the first poems I wrote was just after his birth and it tells of how I felt at that time:

SEPTEMBER 22

There was a chill in the air,
The trees were near bare,
And the sky was cold and grey.
A sadness fell o'er my entire world
On that fateful September day.
That day should have been full of happiness,
A day of hope and joy,
When the news was announced to everyone
That I had a baby boy.

All mothers who are expecting a child
Have dreams of what will be.
They plan for the future life to come,
A life they feel but can't see.
It should have been a day of cheer,
That bleak September day.
But my life collapsed before my eyes—
All my dreams were taken away.
The news that came to fall on my ears
And near took my breath away—
My little son was a Mongoloid,
And my whole life was changed that day.
As the weeks rolled by and a new year came neigh,
My sorrow was somehow relieved.

Now I had grown to love this child
More than I could ever believe.

—December 1967

4

THE JOURNAL

The first entry in the journal was:

"3 weeks—John turns over from his stomach to his back. He 'scoots' all over his bed. I have had trouble with detergent burn in the diaper area. I first tried A & D ointment but it seemed to make it worse. Next I used Zinc Oxide ointment, which helped a little, and finally I changed to Dreft washing powder for diapers. This has cleared the rash."

"7 weeks—First visit to Dr. Eto—weight 12 lbs. 6oz, 24" long."

"2 months—Smiled for the first time. Seems to know me and prefers women to men. He has a very strong grasp. Can hold rattle but does not have control of dropping or turning loose of objects."

The first page of the journal read like this…

John Albert was born September 22, 1967 at 3:20 A.M. in St. Mary's Hospital, Clayton, Missouri. Doctor E.G. Hamilton, M.D. delivered him. Sister Richard Marie was head nurse of the Nursery. Dr. Jackson K, Eto was called on the case to confirm the baby was Mongoloid.

John has a weakness and lack of control of his neck muscles. The palms of his hands have one line all the way across. They call it a "simian crease." His body seems a little long for his legs. He measures 21" in length and weighed 6 lbs. 3 oz. at birth. There is no bridge in his nose, giving him a "flattish" look with a "pug" nose. He has quite a bit of mucus. His ears are very small and his fingers are a little short as are his legs.

I have decided to keep this record of the progress, illnesses, treatments and reactions of John and perhaps one day this might be of help to another mother in caring for her Down Syndrome child."

The journal goes on describing each new happening in John's life….

4 months, laughed aloud. He is fascinated with his hands and holds them over his head for long periods of time. He has slept all night since he was 6 weeks old, taking a short nap in the morning and from one to two hours in the afternoon. He turns from back to stomach. Has had a cold and sore throat and is taking anti-biotic. He keeps choking on mucus.

5-1/2 months he weighs 15lbs 8 oz. and is 26-1/2" long. He seems to be in good health. My hope is that he can sit at 9 months but I really doubt it. My guess would be 1 year unless he starts to progress more. Each day he seems to slow down more. His progress has nearly stopped since he was 4 months. His features are much more pronounced than they were at birth, especially when he is not smiling. For the first time, I noticed he has only two joints in each of his little fingers. Also, he has developed rough, almost calloused, patches of skin on the sides of his hands and the bottoms and sides of his feet. I have found that soaking these areas in water and rubbing briskly with towels, and then using baby magic or other oils makes these areas softer and almost unnoticeable.

8 mo. May 30, 1968. John went on his first picnic. He was so good and never cried. He won a gift certificate for being the youngest one there…His feelings are easily hurt and loud noises or confusion makes him cry and he is hard to calm down. He weighs nearly 20 lbs.

8-½ months. Decided to change doctors. Dr. Eto doesn't really seem to care about John. We are going to Dr. Peter Danis who has experience with Downs children. He found that John was anemic. Had his first earache. Temp was 104°. Went to Cardinal Glennon Hospital where Dr. Quiltie gave him medicine and prescriptions. He has cut two teeth on the bottom.

10 months. John loves to ride in a stroller. We strap him into an infant seat and that is strapped to the stroller. He has become very attached to Hibby, my oldest son. He prefers certain toys over others. He sits upright in his infant seat to eat. He eats foods from the table, loves ice cream or sweets of any kind. He has a good appetite. His head seems to be getting more flat in back as he is in one position lying down most of the time.

12 mos. John learned to 'patty cake'. He has three teeth and tries to crawl. Rides in his stroller without his infant seat. Sits in his high chair to

eat. At first he had trouble sitting without toppling over. Wrote another poem about John as I see him now:

JOHN

How happy he is just lying there
In his crib-like little bed.
He doesn't know of the world outside
Or the many tears I've shed.

How glad he seems to be alive
As he babbles on and on.
And only God know of my aching heart
As I watch my little son, John.

For the little child whose mind is slow
Our world is much too great.
He only knows of simple things.
He knows not of his fate.

With soft white skin, he's lying there,
And my heart fills with pride.
Such laughing eyes and corn silk hair,
He's content just to be alive.

Yet I cannot help but sometimes wonder
What troubles wait for him?
The little son who is so different…
My heart cries out for all of them.

What does he have to offer us?
The little child who's slow.
He has his overwhelming love,
A love that grows and grows.

He has a smile when we are sad,
A twinkle in his eye,
That seems to say—"Look up, look up,
Have faith in God, Don't cry."

He has a joy of little things,
His hands, his toes, his feet.
A great big smile and patty cake
For everyone we meet.

No one knows, like a mother knows,
As each day of life unfolds,
The tender love of a little child....
Whose mind just never grows.

—October, 1968

15. mo. Christmas. This is the second Christmas for John. He was thrilled with everything—the tree, the train under the tree and his toys. He got a toy piano and xylophone that looks like a typewriter. He loves to bang on them. John has 4 teeth now. About two weeks before Christmas he learned to crawl. Now he goes everywhere. He got a walker for Christmas, also. His delight over Christmas was the "spirit of Christmas" personified. He made this the most memorable day of my life. What a good baby he is. He wears size 3 clothes now. Weighs about 24 lbs. He is truly a blessing and joy to our family. He likes to "finger fight" and "patty cake." He also loves to turn off the light and play the piano. He points to things and says, "DIS" for this. Everything is "Dis" to him.

16 mo. Went to doctor for physical. Weighs 24 lbs 10oz., was 33" in height.

19 mo. April 21st. Started training John for potty. He is catching on very fast. Was trained to hold during the day until put on potty. He had a few accidents. He would tell me he had to "GOP" (go pot) until he had to go to the hospital where no one paid him attention when he told them. He went to the hospital May 29, 1969, first hospital visit. Had a virus with diarrhea and vomiting. Had to be fed intravenously. After he came home from the hospital he went back to holding until he was put on the little potty chair.

2yrs. Sept. 22. Had a real nice birthday. John likes to get presents. All his friends in the neighborhood came for ice cream and cake.

25 mo. Oct. 18th.—John had his first plane trip. We flew from St. Louis to Little Rock. He wasn't the least bit frightened. Really enjoyed himself. He took the flight much better than I did. He made friends with the football player across the aisle from us.

27 mo. Christmas. He really enjoyed everything. He thought he was the center of attention. Went right to his toys like he knew which were his. He likes balls. He's walking around furniture and walls and takes a few steps when coaxed but hasn't quite made up his mind to go out on his own.

29 mos. Feb. 1970. He walks everywhere now. Is into everything. He likes to play with racecars. He hasn't had even a cold this winter.

July 1970. John got a bad cold. We all had it. Also, he had Roseola or 3 day measles. Had fever for three days, then a pink rash very similar to heat rash. He walks every night. Loves to play with neighborhood kids. He says several words now, go, car, bye, two, three, down, dad, mom, shut up. When asked how old are you, he holds up two fingers and says "two." When asked how big are you, he puts both hands on his head and says "this." John plays well with other children. He tries to do what they tell him, likes to please.

Sept. 1970. He understands much more than he can talk or speak. He makes his wants known. He wants to be a big boy—no baby things. I have to force him to drink his bottle. Am going to stop that right away. He hasn't worn a diaper at night since June. Only one accident. He's very embarrassed about doing something wrong. He loves to play ball and throws very good. He watches football and baseball on TV. Also likes programs with dancing and music.

Jan. 1971. Christmas was very exciting for John. We spent Christmas in Little Rock with my parents. He is really a hand full. He tries to play their record player and gets into everything. We took him to see Santa Claus but he didn't like him at all. I think he was afraid of his beard or perhaps it was because he didn't know him.

June 1971. Went to Nashville & Little Rock. Took him to the park and he rode the little cars. He really liked it. Also went to a special park they built for "special" children.

Aug. 1971. Went to Little Rock again and left children. John was very good and didn't seem to miss me but was glad to see me when we got back. My parents took him to the park twice. He sure likes the little cars. He is becoming more self-reliant now. Also uses two words together like, "thank you, Mom-ma." John knows all the parts of his body. He tries to help around the house.

Sept. 1971—4 yrs. Have been trying to get John into a preschool. Had interviews with SLARC. Enrolled him in the La Due school. Next I got a notice of a new 'Readiness School' at the Cure' of Ars church and school on Laclede Station Road. I had an interview with the teacher, Mrs. Mitchell, and she is going to take him on a two-month trial basis. I didn't tell her that he was handicapped until we arrived at the interview. I could tell she was quite surprised but I was lucky that the Priest at this church has a niece with Down Syndrome and he asked her to try John, as a favor to him. Otherwise, I feel she would have turned us down. He starts school Monday, September 13, 1971, from 8:45 to 11:45. Monday, Tuesday and Wednesday each week. This school used the Montessori method of teaching. Sure hope he does well. It will be a break through for all of these special children.

Mrs. Carol Walker helped John for the first few weeks in school. She is a friend of his teacher and has taught exceptional children. She is very good with John. Also a young 20-year-old college boy, Gary Paul, comes three days a week and works with John. He goes to school Mon., Wed., and Fri. now. John really likes Gary. He has adjusted very quickly to school and really likes it. Everyone is very pleased with his progress.

Oct. 20, Oct. 27, 1971. These two days John went to Cardinal Glennon Child Development Clinic at Cardinal Glennon Hospital to be evaluated. John was 4 years, one month old. The following are results of a seven-man team:

"Functioning at approximately 2 yr. level intellectually. Self-help skills at about 3-1/2 year level. Receptive language (understanding) at a 2-2 ½ yr level. Expressive language (speech) at a 2 yr. level.

Diet adequate, recommendations: continue pre-school placement. Continue to encourage self-help skills at home. Speech and language therapy program. Re-evaluation in about 18 mos."

John has started speech therapy two days a week at Glennon Hall, Tuesday and Thursday. He is cooperating beautifully, the teachers say. He seems to be trying to talk more He is putting two or more words together. John had a bad sore throat so really hasn't felt good. He is truly a joy of a child. Everyone makes over him and he eats it up.

Christmas 1971. Four years old. Got a tricycle—we could have forgotten everything else. That's all he wanted. He had a real good day even though he felt bad—had a bad cold.

March 1972. John is doing well in school. He has speech once a week from Mrs. Alice Bante who teaches at St. Louis University. He also has speech at the Child Development Clinic two days per week, 1 hr. per day. His speech has improved and his vocabulary has certainly increased. Although many words are not clear, he tries to give a name to everything. This is most encouraging to me. He puts several words together like "more milk please, my coat, my hand," etc. John has been sick this winter. Nothing very serious, just colds, flu, etc.

June 1972. School is over the last of this month. John has really done well. He is more independent. Goes down a 9 ft. slide by himself. He doesn't want me to hold his hand and he doesn't want me to come to the door for him at school.

July 8. John learned to peddle his tricycle today. Until now he had pushed with his feet but wouldn't peddle. July 13 is the last day for his speech at the Child Development Clinic. The lessons have definitely helped his speech.

Aug. 17, 1972. John was evaluated by the special school district today. He was not in a good humor and was not very cooperative with us but regardless, he tested out in the 'educable' range. I am really very proud of him. Guess our hard work has paid off. He has been assigned to Park School on Eddie and Park Roads. We are going to put him on the bus the second day and see how he does. He won't be five years old until Sept. 22nd. He seems so small to go to school all day. We received the following letter from St. Louis County School System saying John had been accepted and would go to Park School and be in a class for the educable mentally retarded:

HE24456

SPECIAL SCHOOL DISTRICT of St. Louis County, Missouri
9820 Manchester Road, Rock Hill, Missouri 63119
Oral W. Spurgeon, Superintendent   Phone 962-4667

BOARD MEMBERS
Wendell H. Stark, President
Armstrong B. Crider, Vice President
Lillian M. Feller, Secretary
William F. Allison
Mrs. Whitty Cuningsim
J. Thomas Harrington

August 18, 1972

Mr. and Mrs. Albert Wilkat
1212 Selma Avenue
St. Louis, Missouri   63119

RE: WILKAT, JOHN ALBERT
D.O.B.   9-22-67

Dear Parents:

Your child is assigned to a class for the ___educable___ mentally retarded at:

District: SPECIAL   Principal: Mrs. Ruey T. Brooks
School: PARK   Teacher: to be assigned
Address: 9510 Eddie & Park Rd., 63126   Phone: 843-6555

School begins September 5, 1972.

Your child may be transported by Special School District. If eligible, (see paragraph below) our Transportation Office will advise you of exact bus arrangements.

Regulations state that transportation shall be provided for all "Trainable" children served by the Special School District. All other children (all who are not "Trainable") under age 13 are provided transportation only if they live at least one-half mile from their school. If they are above 13 years of age they are transported if they live at least one mile from school.

If eligible for transportation and you want to transport to and from school until arrangements are made, you are free to do so beginning immediately but you must transport the child both ways. If you do not want the child to ride a school bus and prefer to do all the transporting, please call this office so we can record that decision.

Lunch will be available at the school at 40¢ per day. However, a child may bring his own lunch if desired.

In order to keep our files current, we ask that you keep us informed of any changes in home address or telephone number and any other pertinent information that will help us be of further service to your child. We shall be looking forward to having your child in our program and we hope that the year will be pleasant, profitable, and successful. Please feel free to visit the classroom any time at your convenience during the school year and call us if you have any questions.

Sincerely yours,

John W. Kidd, Ed.D.
Assistant Superintendent
Department for the Mentally Retarded

JWK/dmb
cc: Webster Groves
     Home School District

What a happy day that was!

5

PRESCHOOL

When John went to the Montessori school, Cure'of Ars Readiness School, I became involved more with his learning. A trait he had, and carried with him all through his life, was taking everything literally. He didn't have the capacity to determine when it was O K to change the rules. This had its good points and it's bad. When he first started the pre-school, everything went well except Mrs. Mitchell said about the middle of the morning he would begin to cry. She couldn't determine from him what the trouble was. She looked to see if someone was not being nice to him, etc. Finally she came to me with this as it was really weighing on her mind. She said, "He doesn't cry when you leave. It's after awhile, usually when we are going to the playground."

I thought and thought of what this could mean. Then I remembered something that I said to John each morning. "John, you stay right here in this room until Mom comes for you. Don't go anywhere else, O K?" The next day I said to Mrs. Mitchell, "I think I have determined our problem. Let me know how he behaves today." When I left John that day I said, "John, Mom is going home now. You stay with Mrs. Mitchell, wherever she goes. I will pick you up later." That day there were no tears. In my anxiety about John possibly leaving the classroom and wandering off the grounds, (they backed up to some thick wooded areas), I had told him to stay in the room. Then, when Mrs. Mitchell took the children to the playground, he thought that he shouldn't go and started to cry because he was being made to disobey my instructions.

The preschool, and also speech classes, helped John tremendously. At home I made labels for everything so that he could associate words with objects. The idea came to me after a trip to the grocery store. My dad was carrying John through the store and John said, "Papa, Lemon Fresh," and he pointed to a bottle of "JOY" detergent.

My dad was so excited he came hurrying over to me and said, "Melba Jo, watch this. The 'little scudder' recognized a bottle of Joy." We went back and John said the same thing. He had seen the ads on television and put the phrase "Lemon Fresh" with the word, JOY.

I labeled the wall, chairs, table, floor, door, etc. all through our house. One day someone stopped by who didn't know what I was doing and they said, "Is Al drinking a lot these days?" We laughed about this, but it worked and John learned to "read" his first words this way. Later, when he started kindergarten, I made 3 x 5 cards with words on one side and a picture of the word on the other side and used them as flash cards as we waited for his bus in the mornings.

John had a young man who was a college student who came and helped him at the pre-school. His name was Gary Paul. Gary got married the second year and John was invited to the wedding. Another help was a lady named Carol Walker. She was a friend of Mrs. Mitchell and they both had training in Montessori teaching. Carol had an idea that this was the way handicapped and mentally challenged children should all be taught and she opened a preschool for the mentally handicapped. John stayed in the room with Mrs. Mitchell and I helped out in the "free" school for handicapped that Carol started. This is when I was introduced to other types of handicaps like Cerebral Palsy, brain damage from unknown sources and also Autism. I never realized how many things could happen to make a child mentally challenged. This would help me later when I would need to help get resources these children required in their learning process.

Carol was a funny person. She always felt that God spoke to us. The problem was we never listened. But Carol did. I recall driving to a meeting with the Knights of Columbus where we were going to make a plea for their financial help. All of a sudden Carol pulled over to the curb and began praying, ALOUD. I really didn't know what to do or say, as I had never been around anyone who was so 'obvious' with their beliefs. We had delayed our trip a couple of days before because she had a flat tire and felt God was telling us this was not the right time. As it turns out, she was right. It wasn't the right time because the person who was our best advocate didn't make that meeting. Since we waited, he was there at the meeting we attended and spoke for our cause and we received financial help. Carol never took one cent of pay for her time. As I look back now, even then, John's presence on earth was making a difference. And now I think, maybe Carol was really right. God works in mysterious ways. That pre-school went on for many years and it was free to those who attended. They took children who couldn't get into any other program. Carol always felt that the pre-school was meant to be for another reason. The church, Cure'of Ars, was named for a priest in a very small village in France named Ars. Cure' meant priest or instructor. This priest was slow, mentally, and never went any farther in his priesthood than this little village. He was a young man with limited intelligence whose greatest desire was to be a priest and he overcame many challenges. This church had built a school addition, and for one reason or another it had not worked out so the classrooms stood empty until Mrs. Mitchell rented one to hold her Montessori school. Then, later, Carol somehow talked the church into giving her school a room also.

Carol was a friend of Alice Bante, who was the instructor at St. Louis University and head of the speech therapy program. Through them, a speech therapy program for pre-school mentally handicapped children was established. This had not been tried before and students who attended St. Louis University majoring in speech therapy donated their time giving therapy to these children. The students received credit towards their degree for their time and the children received much needed therapy. It was a 'WIN-WIN' situation. My feelings were, and still are, the sooner you start teaching these children, the easier it is for them to learn. The more they know before entering school, the better it is for them.

Case in point...A lady approached Carol about the school. Her family was considering putting their three-year-old Down Syndrome daughter into a home, as she was becoming too much trouble to care for. Carol asked to let her come to the school for a month and see what we could do. This little girl had several brothers and sisters who did everything for her. The parents still had her eating creamed baby food and she took a bottle.

She could not sit, stand, walk, was not toilet trained and was a total care for every little thing. The first day we did not realize that she didn't eat 'real' food and gave her a piece of apple. She started to choke before it occurred to us that she had no idea of how to chew. From then on, we treated her as a new born. Carol spent hours with this child, but before the month was over, the little girl could and did eat real food. She was standing on her own and starting to take steps and was beginning to make sounds, trying to say words. Can you imagine how this family felt? You have never seen people who were so thrilled. While they had done everything for this child thinking they were helping her, they were, in fact, holding her back. She had not been challenged or encouraged.

One thing I found out about children with Down Syndrome is that they are a little on the lazy side and take the path of least resistance. You have to encourage them constantly and peak their interest in everything. When John was a baby, I had a place in every room for him. I borrowed playpens. They were in every room and each one had something different to look at or play with. I tried to get his attention on something different each day. During the cold days, I would hold him up to the window so he could see outside. I talked to him constantly and my other children followed suit. We all tried to keep his mind focusing on new things, new smells, new touches, and new sights. I still believe this had lots to do with his later mental ability. None of us ever uses our full potential or "I.Q." We wanted John to get as much as he could from his. John did not disappoint us.

6

SUPPORT GROUP

Right after John was born, a lady named Sarah Young contacted me. She was a friend of a lady I met at a Tupperware Party. Sarah had a young son, named Brian, who had Down Syndrome. She reached out to me when I truly needed a friend who was experiencing what I was. We became close friends and it was at this time that the two of us joined a group of women at their second meeting. These were mothers with children who had Down Syndrome. The first meeting they had only a handful of people attend. The second meeting, however, and the one I first went to, there were about 39 ladies there. We decided on the name of M & M's, which stood for Mothers of Mongoloids (as that is what these children were called at that time).

We met once a month, first at different homes and then, by the second year, we started meeting at the County Health Department. It was mostly a support group where we exchanged ideas with others. It was a big help to me as I was introduced to people like Pearl Nelson. Her son, Chris, was older, a teenager, and she had been through so much with schools, etc. and she was a wealth of information. She became the "President" of our little organization and her help was a gift to all of us who had small children. Sarah and I used to go to the meetings together.

At Christmas, we would have a party for all the children (they were all ages) and Santa was there with gifts and also hamburgers, chips, and drinks. It was amusing to watch these kids...they looked related to each other. When you would stand back and watch them, they looked like brothers and sisters, even more so than they did with their biological brothers and sisters. It was their faces, I think, more than anything else.

The personalities were similar, too. Very easy going and they all seemed to enjoy being together.

The M & M's branched out and started an outreach program to include visitation to hospitals when other babies were born with Down Syndrome. We would visit the mothers and welcome them to our group and give them whatever help they needed. It could be touchy sometimes. There were times when perhaps the mother didn't want to accept what had happened and I could truly relate to that. If you don't acknowledge it, it isn't there!!! Denial is one of the first things that hit a new mother. After acceptance, however, they usually ended up with us.

We also were instrumental in getting legislature passed in Jefferson City, Missouri's state capitol. I recall one time we rented a bus and went to Jefferson City to a meeting which didn't take place until almost 11:00 P.M. The legislature was over-whelmed at the turnout from our group and some people had to stand in the hall. The bill passed and we were happy about that. Later a national bill very much like this one was passed at the national level. Basically the bill said, "every child must be educated to the ability of that individual child." In other words, you could not lump them together, saying no Cerebral Palsy child can get this or no Down Syndrome child can be in an educable class. Every child must be tested and educated according to that child's ability.

The M & M's, which started out as a rather small group of women, has continued on all these many years. It was 36 years ago when I first went to a meeting at the home of one of the original seven mothers. That was the second meeting and over 35+ people were there. The term 'Mongoloid' has long since been dropped, in referring to these children, and has been replaced with Down Syndrome, named for John Langdon Down, who in 1866 published a medical paper describing most accurately some of the characteristics of this syndrome. Keeping up with the times, the organization changed the name to Down Syndrome Association of Greater St. Louis and today they have their own website. They continue to reach out to new mothers and their babies helping them to cope with what life has in store for them. Things are so much better now than they were 36 years ago, so many doors have been opened, so many changes made. I like to think that John had a small part in this revolution.

7

HIS DAY ON TV

One time, when John was about 4 years old, I was called upon to be on a local TV show with John. It was a "Telethon For Forgotten Children," which was held at the Chase Hotel. The telethon was to make money by donations from people who watched and called in their pledges. It lasted 24 hours and there were several celebrities who lent their names and positions to this cause. John and I were scheduled to appear on Sunday afternoon but we were to go to the hotel around noon. We waited in a hotel room they had for us and when the time came near to our appearance, we were moved to the stage area. There was a sofa there that we sat on. It was located very near the edge of the stage. All of a sudden, Jackie Cooper came to where I was seated and held up his hand and said, "Hello, I'm Jackie Cooper."

I said, "Yes, I know who you are," and we shook hands. With that, John held out his hand, but he was on the other side of me so it was impossible for him to shake hands.

Without hesitation, Jackie Cooper jumped upon the stage and took his hand and said, "Bless your heart. I want to shake your hand, too." John had no idea who he was, or of his importance, he just knew he liked him.

The man who interviewed us was named Jack Smith. He, also, was a performer and had a TV show named "You Asked For It." I don't remember what they did but he wasn't nearly as personable as Jackie Cooper. I had thought of all the questions he might ask me and the answers I might give. I never in a million years thought of the question he did ask which was, "How did you feel when you found out you had a Down Syndrome child?"

Now what kind of question is that to ask someone? I answered that I felt pretty much like anyone else would feel. Later, in the interview, he asked about where John went to school and I told him about the Montessori school. He said "Why would you send him to a place where the other children were functioning above him?"

To this I answered, "If you want to learn how to play tennis, do you play with a beginner or someone who knows how to play well?" He agreed that you would learn more by playing with a good tennis player and probably learn more by being with those more intelligent than you.

John looked so cute that day. He had on a long sleeved red velvet shirt with long blue pants and his blonde hair was cut like the little doughboy. That was the way kids wore their hair then, long hair for boys. It made John look so cute. I still have pictures of him wearing that outfit, and each time I look at them, I can remember that precious little face and the day we had our TV debut.

T.V. Debut

8

FIRST SCHOOL

John started kindergarten at Park Elementary school. It was a special education school for both the mentally and physically challenged. His teacher was a beautiful lady named Mrs. Bartelt (pronounced Bartell). Not only was she beautiful on the outside with long blonde hair and an angel face, she was just as beautiful on the inside. Mrs. Bartelt had a brother with Down Syndrome so she really had a soft spot in her heart for the children who were mentally challenged. All of the children worshipped her. John would refer to his teacher as 'Bartell'. I never did know why he left off the Mrs. He fell in love with his teacher right off. It was truly a great experience for John, being his first time to be away from home by himself all day. On top of that, he had to ride a bus to school, as it was several miles from our house. There again he was very lucky to have the bus driver that he did. Her name was Mrs. Harris. She took such good care of those children, almost as if they were her very own kids. I never had to worry about John while he was in the care of these two ladies.

Somehow I got talked into being the 'room' mother. I had gotten to know Mrs. Bartelt pretty well as I went to school often. I enjoyed being room mother because I had gotten to know this teacher from first hand experience. As room mother, I was in charge of the parties that they had on special occasions. At the first PTA meeting, which took place about two months after school started, it was my job to introduce Mrs. Bartelt. I wanted to make it a special introduction for this exceptional lady so I spent some time thinking of how to make this happen. Finally, I came up with the idea of writing a poem about her. Here it is:

MRS. BARTEL

Since September 6th of this year, I've had a second mother.
A pretty lady with golden hair—I'd trade her for no other.
Some of the children call her teacher. They don't know her name too well.
But I know her name some better, so I call her Bartelt.

She teaches us the alphabet, and how to read and write.
She praises us for being good, but scolds us when we fight.
The children in my class, you see, are sometimes called retarded.
But no one knows the outcome of the knowledge she has started.

Some folks would like to turn their head—or put us all away.
But Bartelt has faith in what we do, and shows it everyday.
She makes us feel like we belong and each one has a place.
She loves each child in her whole class and it shows on her face.

She's an angel sent from heaven, to help the special child.
Her presence gives strength to the weak; her voice can tame the wild.
How can we ever thank her for all that she has done?
She gives our lives new meaning and makes living much more fun.

I wish that I could tell her how much she means to me.
How much her help and guidance has shaped what I will be.
I pray that God in Heaven will bless her with His love.
And that her life will always be watched over from above.

I ended it with, "Ladies and Gentlemen, it is my special privilege to present to you, our children's teacher, Mrs. Sue Bartelt." There was a round of applause and she had tears in her eyes when she approached the stage.

Mrs. Bartelt started John's schooling on a high note and from then on he enjoyed going to school.

Every morning we waited outside our house for the school bus, and to make it a little more interesting, I made index cards with new words for him to learn. On the back I would put a picture of the word. If he couldn't get the word, I would show him the back side and little by little he learned new words. One day, while I was visiting the school, I noticed a pretty little girl who seemed very bright. She seemed to learn so quickly and I spoke to the teacher about this asking why it took John so long to learn something and she seemed to grasp it immediately. I remarked how I wished John could learn more quickly. Mrs. Bartelt told me that while I might think this child was quicker than John, and obviously she was, that she had no retention. One day she might learn that C-A-T spelled cat, the following day, when asked the same question, she would smile and say, dog, or something else like that. She explained that this little girl was brain damaged and could not retain information so it had to be repeated over and over and over. By the same token, it would take John three or four times as long to learn that C-A-T was cat but once he learned it, he never forgot. John's brain was like a trap, once something got into it, it never got out. That was a trait that he continued to have forever. She said she wished all the children were more like John. She felt discouraged when this little girl could not remember what she had worked so hard to teach her. With John, once he knew it, he knew it, and she would feel a sense of accomplishment and pride.

The school year passed quickly and we came to the end of the year with these two special ladies, Mrs. Bartelt and Mrs. Harris. I felt that I needed to do something a little extra for Mrs. Harris, who had done the almost impossible of driving these children to school through snow and rain and she made them feel so secure. I bought her a little gift and card of thanks and I wrote a poem that I included in the card. Mrs. Harris continued to drive the bus John rode until we moved to Florida. I have often wished I had kept in touch with her.

Those first years we had in St. Louis were very important ones and things that both John and I learned would follow us through our lives.

Following is the poem I wrote for this very caring woman who drove the school bus. I wonder if she ever knew how important her role had been in my son's life.

MRS. HARRIS

Let me tell you of my special friend,
A lady very strong.
She drives us kids to school each day.
Sometimes the ride is long.

Each child who gets aboard her bus
She helps with tender care.
She talks to us and jokes with us
Until our bus gets there.

With dancing eyes and a great big smile
She greets us everyday.
Then drives our yellow bus to school
So we can learn and play.

The children who ride bus 104,
Are different, every one.
Some crippled, some retarded, but—
She makes our life more fun.

To her it doesn't seem to matter
how handicapped we are.
Each one is like her very own—
Her special shining star.

In rain and snow, in sleet and hail,
She's always on the go.
Loading wheel chairs, watching closely,
Helping ones who're slow.

Our safety is her main concern
So in our seats we sit.
She drives the bus so carefully
That some girls even knit.

Each night now when I say my prayers
I ask the Lord above,
"Dear Lord, please bless Mrs. Harris.
She drives our bus with love."

—December, 1973

9

CARNIVAL DAY AT PARK SCHOOL

Park Elementary School had a very active Parents group. This school was for exceptional children with either or both mental handicaps or physical handicaps. The children interacted and became familiar with each other's handicap. There was one little girl that went to the school who was a Thalidomide baby. Thalidomide is a drug that originated in Switzerland and was used as a mild sedative. It was banned in the United States, for the most part, after it became suspect in causing a congenital deformity in babies when pregnant mothers took the sedative. This deformity, called phocomelia, causes the babies to be born with hands and/or feet being attached to the trunk or body by single, very short bones. It was my understanding that this little girl's mother was living in Germany while the father was stationed there, and she took this drug when she was pregnant. The child had both arms and legs effected and she was pretty much a little body with hands coming out of her shoulders and her feet coming from her lower body. It was not a pretty sight and, when seeing her for the first time, it could take your breath. She maneuvered herself around the school on a little cart someone had made for her. It looked like a small sled with rollers, about 6 inches off the ground. She would lie on her belly, face down, holding her head up, and push herself with the two little hands that projected from her shoulders at the end of a very, very small little bone or arm. She could speed around the halls so fast the others had to watch out for her. It was truly amazing.

The parents group, each year, funded an all day affair at the school that had sort of a circus or carnival theme. They would have all sorts of rides,

Ferris wheels, ponies, little car rides and always clowns and all types of carnival foods, hot dogs, hamburgers, ice cream, pop corn, cotton candy, all kinds of goodies. Everything was on the school grounds and it was something that the kids looked forward to each year. The first year John went we were new to the school and really didn't know what to expect. I was as excited as the kids, I think. I went that day, since I was the room mother, and also, I wanted to be with John during this experience. We were walking around looking at everything and admiring all the events when out of the corner of my eye, I spotted this little Thalidomide girl. I hadn't seen her before, however, I had heard about her. I started trying to steer John in the other direction, not wanting him to see her and perhaps it upsetting him. I found it hard to look at her without staring at the obvious, and I didn't want this for him. But before I knew it, John grabbed my hand and started pulling me towards this girl. She was braced up in a wheel chair so she didn't fall over, since her balance wasn't so good in an upright position, as she had no legs to keep her from falling forward. John said, "Come Mom, Come here and see." He was pulling me and without making a scene I had to go with him. He hurried over and said, "Hello, there!"

I almost gasped, and I remember thinking, he doesn't even notice that she doesn't have arms and legs. Then he said, "Mom, this is my good friend. Look Mom, no arms and no legs." He smiled and hugged her, and off he went, like nothing was unusual. He made me feel so small, so ashamed that day. Again, looking through his eyes, he only saw his friend. That she had no arms and no legs meant nothing to him, it was just a fact of life. He saw the little girl inside, and she was his friend. Those words would ring in my ears forever, "Look Mom, no arms and no legs, this is my friend."

Top-Playing around with Judy and Tom.
Bottom-John and Dad, waiting for school bus.

10

THE MOVE TO FLORIDA

In 1974, John started having a little trouble walking and after awhile he started falling. We took him to the doctor and he was tested and finally, Dr. Peter Danis sent us to Dr. O'Reilly, an Orthopedist, to get his opinion. This led us to John's first operation. He was operated on in May, 1974. It was called a "Grice Procedure." Basically, they took bone from his left leg and put it into his left foot, which worked as a wedge to push his foot into a more upright position. He was walking on the arch of his foot, throwing the foot out to the side. This operation took place in Cardinal Glennon Hospital in St. Louis.

It was just about this time that my husband was notified he was being transferred to Florida. Now things were changing for all of us, and especially for John. He would be leaving everything familiar to him and going into the unknown. We made our move to Florida right after the beginning of the school year, October 4, 1974.

This move to Florida was a difficult one for the family. It was especially difficult for Judy and Tom, as she was in Middle School and he in High School. They had lived in Missouri and the same house all their lives. Both had been born when we lived on Selma Street and they had long time friends that they were forced to leave behind. Our son, Hibby, would stay behind as he was in college and didn't want to make the change. There was an empty feeling as we drove to our new home. All our furniture, indeed everything we possessed, was somewhere between Missouri and Florida and we had neither a home in Missouri nor a home in Florida. We were truly 'in limbo'. Judy started crying almost immediately as we pulled away from Selma Street. To make matters worse, it started to rain on us about half way. Our station wagon looked like gypsies were inside as we had luggage on top of the station wagon, plants, etc. in the back of the station wagon, a broom was tied to the top and inside were five humans, two dogs, a cat and a turtle. The animals were nervous about the trip because none of them had actually ridden in an automobile except to go to the Vets to get check ups and shots and they had only bad memories of previous car rides. It took us almost three days to reach our new home, and those were very long and trying days for us all.

We felt so bad that the kids were unhappy and there just wasn't much we could say or do to make them feel better. Al, Tom and John sat in the front seat with John sitting between his father and brother. I sometimes wonder what John was feeling about this journey that he didn't understand. To him, it was just an adventure. He didn't understand the concept of 'moving and not returning'. That wasn't so with the other two. While Tom wasn't as obvious with his grief as Judy, he sat looking straight ahead and spoke very little. Judy just sobbed. There was no consoling her. The animals were moving about the car from one spot to another, it was raining outside and I was wondering if we would ever make it to Florida. There was also speculation as to whether there was more water outside the car or inside the car between the tears and the rain.

Myeoshi, our Siamese cat was really nervous. She was walking around and around the car, from the back seat to the front seat, round and round, and then she started going from the back seat to the top of the front seat, going in a circle all the while going Meow! Meow! Meow! It was really sad. All of a sudden she was walking on the back of the front seat, behind John's head, Meow! Meow! Meow! With that, John turned around and with his hand he shoved her backside, pushing her into the back of the car and at the same time saying, "Meow, my butt. Go away!" This brought laughter to all of us and sort of broke the 'ice' as far as the move was concerned. The sun finally came out and we were on our way to our new life.

Plantation, Florida…it was certainly different. Plantation is a suburb of the city of Ft. Lauderdale and is located approximately 30 miles north of Miami. My husband's new office was located in Miami but because of the school situation, we chose Plantation to be our home. It was almost in the country and within blocks of us cows grazed in pastures. There was very little traffic, except for the local traffic, and we chose a house on a street that was off the beaten path. With John walking around and so much going on in our lives, we didn't want the added aggravation of worrying that a car might hit him. The street we moved to had several children living there and a couple of them were John's age. Everyone tried to make us feel at home. Judy and Tom made friends with the neighbors across the street, who were very close to their age. Those friends introduced our kids to others that they would go to school with so it made the transition a little more tolerable.

Several of the children would play with John, on occasion, but you could see that he was not able to keep up with them. One of our neighbors, and a very good friend of mine, invited John to her son's birthday party. I hesitated on letting him go but not wanting to hurt anyone's feelings, I said he could attend and I would help her with the party. Everything went well for a while. There were about eight or ten little boys there, all about John's age. Then they went into the back yard to play, running around and having fun. Billie, my friend, and I watched from the window. John was running like the others and they were all laughing and having fun. All of a sudden John stopped; he looked around and then sat down in the middle of the yard, put his face in his hands and started crying. This was possibly the first time that John realized that he wasn't quite like the other boys. Always before, he had been with children who had limits also, or when he was with 'normal' children, there was always adult supervision. On his own, with his own peers, he just couldn't quite make it. It was obvious, even Billie said, "I think he has first realized he's not like the others." From that time on, I never left him without an adult to supervise when he was with other children. He learned to play alone, and as he grew older, he seemed to prefer to be alone and entertain himself. Even in school, he was pretty much 'a loner', which I thought was very sad.

Looking into all places to locate, we decided on the little town named Plantation, mainly because it offered better schooling than the other places we looked. For one thing neither my daughter, Judy, nor my son, Tom, would have to ride a bus to school. Judy was in Middle School and Tom in High School and it was important to me that they not have to ride a bus.

One child riding a bus was totally enough and John would surely have to ride a bus. It was not clear yet where John would go to school. Broward County, and all of Florida, has a little different setup with their schools than St. Louis County where we were from. In St. Louis, the 'special education department' had its own school board, whereas in Florida, everyone fell into the same category with one school board for all. It was to their advantage to have things this way as money allocated to schools was determined by the children that school had enrolled. For example, John had both a physical and mental handicap so the school received money for him being a child, money for a physical handicap and money for a mental handicap. He was quite a score for whatever school he was assigned. The principal of each school then doled out the money the way they saw fit. If no one complained, the majority of the money went to the education of the 'normal' children. New books went to them and the old ones were given to the 'Special Ed' classes. They will all deny this, but that is exactly how it worked. Most parents could have cared less. Their child was out of sight and out of mind. They were just grateful that someone else took care of them for eight hours a day.

All transcripts for my children had been sent to Florida weeks prior to our arriving and the kids being enrolled. With Tom and Judy, we had no problem in their starting school on the Monday after we arrived. John, on the other hand, was another problem. He was being assigned to go into a trainable class. No Down Syndrome children had ever been assigned to 'educable' class. I spoke with the woman in charge (the guidance counselor of the school John would have gone to had he been normal) and she kept telling me I should put John into class and when they got to it, he would be tested and then assigned to a permanent school. It seemed that all of their Psychologists were busy and no one was available to give John a test. Well, I didn't fall off the turnip truck yesterday!!

I knew if they ever once placed him in a trainable class, it would be hell getting him out. Finally, a couple of weeks later, after I had called almost every day, I phoned the Guidance Counselor and said, "I would like the correct spelling of your name to give to our attorney." She asked why and I told her we were filing suit against Broward County Schools and against her because they were not educating my son to his ability. I let her know that not only was I aware of the federal law they were breaking, I helped getting it into place. This was around eight A.M. She said before you do anything; let me get back with you. It was only a few minutes that she phoned back asking me to have John at her school at 10 A.M. She suddenly found someone available to give John a test.

We went there and a very nice man greeted us. He asked John a couple of questions. One was the color of three crayons, red, yellow and blue. Then he asked John to go across the room, open the door, close the door and return to his seat. John got up, went across the room, the door was locked. He tried several times and it would not open. Embarrassed, the man said, "O K, just come sit down." He then said, "Yes, he is educable, and we will get him into a class immediately."

I said, "Is that it? Now would you like to see what he actually knows? Give him one of those readers on the desk, open it to any page, and have him read it to you."

He looked at me like I was nuts, but he got one and opened it. John read it, one word at a time, but he read it. The man could not believe that he had seen this. He said to me, "Are you sure he has Down Syndrome? I have never seen anyone with Down Syndrome his age who could read."

I assured him that "Yes, John had Down Syndrome and he was not unique, that there were many children in St. Louis schools who could do the same, and that I didn't feel that it was because they were from St. Louis, I felt it was because their schooling started at a very early age." John was in a school classroom at Pine Ridge Elementary school before noon that very day.

His teacher was Miss Smith. It was her very first assignment since she got her teacher's degree. There were eight children in the classroom, each one with a different problem. John's education was starting and so was mine!!

About a week later, I got a note from the Middle School asking my permission to have Judy tested. I could not believe that she was having trouble but I signed the permission slip and took her to the school the next Saturday morning. I was to pick her up at noon. I waited outside the school until she came out and to my surprise there was a man walking with her and talking to her. I got out of the car and called her name. She said, "Hi Mom, this is the psychologist who gave me my test. I'm going to be in the "Gifted Class."

He took one look at me and said, "Didn't I just test your son at Mirror Lakes Grade school?"

I said, "Yes, you did. He was the little boy with Down Syndrome."

He said, "You certainly do have unusual children. Not only did your son break all the records, your daughter just made the highest grade we recorded this year."

Later, my neighbor, Ginny Allen, would refer to John as "The GIFTED Mongoloid." It sort of became a joke around the neighborhood. So John was in a classroom for the educable children and Judy was in classes for gifted children...yes, I certainly did have unusual children. I just felt it was a shame he didn't get to test Tommy. He probably would have fainted, as Tom has a pretty high I.Q also.

John's class was in a school where all the other classes had normal children, except his. His teacher was new to the 'business' and so I went often to lend my help in any way I could. One day, she brought my attention a boy named Ronnie who sat under his desk. He had some kind of brain damage and she couldn't reach him with words. All the children knew not to get too close to him because he would bite them. So she just let him sit where he wanted to sit.

I told her, "That's not right. He can't learn anything there, and on top of that, he was making the other children feel uncomfortable, so they were not getting as much as they can from their schooling."

She said she had spoken with her supervisor and was pretty much told to live with it. She said the supervisor would be making her monthly visit any day and she wished I would speak with her. I agreed to do just that. A couple of days later the supervisor showed up. I asked her if I might speak with her, and she said O K. I told her about Ronnie and that I felt he needed to be placed somewhere else. To this she said, "Do you have some sort of training to evaluate this boy? He is exactly where he needs to be and nothing will be changed."

I replied, "No, I haven't had any training to evaluate Ronnie, but I haven't had ice skating lessons either, and I do recognize it when someone falls on their butt. I just don't feel that it is to anyone's benefit to have him sitting under his desk and biting anyone who comes near him."

I turned and walked away. A few minutes later, it was music time and a music teacher came to the room to play for the children. I said to Miss Smith, "Come on, we can take a break. I'm sure that this lady can supervise while we're away." So we left the supervisor with the class and the music teacher. I guess to show us that she knew more than we did the supervisor pulled Ronnie from under the desk and onto her lap. We went to the teacher's lounge and had coffee. About five minutes later, we heard screaming and ran to the room. Ronnie had bitten the supervisor, brought blood, and was back under the desk. Miss Smith apologized to her and said it wouldn't happen again, but that she shouldn't have tried to get him out. The next day Ronnie was reassigned to another school. We never had any more trouble from then on.

That year was my learning period, as far as mental handicaps were concerned. One mother came by and we were talking and I made the comment that it was nice that there was a class for these children. She said, "What do you mean? Nothing is wrong with my daughter." I couldn't believe that she didn't see what was so obvious to everyone else. She said, "What do you think is wrong with her?"

I said, "Well, I was not a doctor, but I would guess that she's autistic." Hearing this, she was horrified. She couldn't believe that I thought this of her daughter. I tried to tell her that I wasn't trying to hurt her feelings, it was just my observation, and obviously something was wrong with her or she wouldn't be in this class. Later that week, she went to her doctor and told him what I had said. He didn't realize that no one had told her of this problem and he had just assumed she knew. She later apologized to me and said she wished she had met me sooner, that I was the only person who had been truthful with her. We talked many times after that and I tried to help her with understanding different problems she had. I told her about how we had encouraged John as a young baby, and I think it helped her to be able to talk about her daughter, to someone who understood.

One day I suggested to Miss Smith that maybe she should teach the children how to pronounce letters of the alphabet, so that they could begin to learn to read. So far they had been coloring pictures and doing very little academically, and this worried me. I knew this was not a familiar zone for her and that she was getting acclimated to each child's handicap. After a couple of days, she told me that she was going to start teaching the letters of the alphabet. She started with A, E, I, O and U. After everyone was thoroughly confused, I suggested to her that perhaps she should first start with consonants rather than vowels, since they only had one sound, whereas, the vowels could have more than one sound. It only seemed natural to me, but she seemed very puzzled by my thinking that, however, we did go to the one sound letters the next day.

I tried to work with children other than John as I felt that he could learn more from someone other than me. It was a challenge and I did enjoy it.

One day I noticed John on the playground and he seemed to be in an argument with a little black girl. I hurried over to see what the problem was, as this special class had playground time with the normal children and close attention had to be paid that no one was hurt. I said, "What's the problem here?"

She said, "He says I'm purple. I'm not purple! I'm brown."

John said, "No she's not, she's purple." I hurried John off and made him say he was sorry, but you know when the sun hit her skin, she did look purple. John always said exactly what he thought, and I had to admit that he did seem to be right.

That first Christmas in Florida, John got a Big Wheel, which is sort of like a tri-cycle except it's made of hard plastic and sits very low to the ground, so that falling off would be difficult. The Big Wheel, if you have ever seen one, made a rather distinct noise when you rode it, sort of a popping noise. I guess you could make the noise stop if you wanted to, but we liked it because we always knew where John was. Our street, 7th street, is two blocks long and the two side streets which attach to 6th court are each one block long, making the entire trip, two blocks down 7th, and two blocks down 6th court, and a block on each end. John could ride his Big

Wheel for six blocks without stopping or having to get into the street. We had always emphasized to John the importance of NOT GOING INTO THE STREET. He was very good about obeying us. John had started making his rounds on his Big Wheel, going counter clock wise around the blocks. He could not be encouraged to change that, always counter clock-wise. When he was on 6th Court we could hear him by the popping of his little vehicle. One day, John came home crying like his heart would break. I could hardly get him to tell me his problem. Finally, he took my hand and led me around the block. There was the problem! Someone on the other street had parked their car so that it blocked the sidewalk, and the only way around was to go into the street. His little Big Wheel was parked right by that car. John couldn't rationalize that it might be O K, just this one time, to go a little into the street to get around the car. He couldn't turn around, because then he would be going the wrong way (clock wise), so he just got off and walked home, crying all the way.

John always tried to do as he was told. He wasn't one to venture out on his own or try to make decisions, and he would try to follow instructions to the letter of the law. You really had to watch what you told him, and try to see things like he saw them.

John lost his front teeth.

After Operation in Florida   Waiting for bus

John with his new puppy, Bo

John with his sister, Judy

11

CHANGING SCHOOLS

In December 1974, John had a second operation on his left foot, as the first one didn't seem to help. His foot would not move up and down and he started having cramps in the calf of his leg and in his foot. We had been recommended to a Dr. John Mahoney, and he did the second Grice procedure on John's left foot, at which time he cut a tendon, to allow the foot to move up and down. In March of 1975, he put John into a leg brace from the knee to the foot. About this time, John's other leg started doing the same thing, and Dr. Mahoney put his right leg into a brace also. Now he was in leg braces on both legs.

When school started, in September 1975, John was reassigned to Plantation Elementary School and his teacher was a Mrs. Goldstein. This was basically the same situation as before, a Special Ed class located in an elementary school for normal children. Mrs. Goldstein had much more to offer John than he had the year before. She had taught special children for several years and was a firm disciplinarian, but a likable, cheerful person. I had started working part time for Sears about that same time. At Christmas, I noticed that the school was decorated for the holidays with pictures on the windows of classrooms and doors, except the room that John was in. It had nothing at all.

I couldn't understand this, and spoke with Mrs. Goldstein about it, asking why they didn't seem to have anything to indicate the holiday. Mrs. Goldstein informed me that she was Jewish and didn't believe in having Santa, etc. or anything that would be associated with Christmas. I told her that I fully understood that, but that none of the children were Jewish and they didn't understand why they couldn't have decorations too.

I just couldn't get this off my mind and I mentioned it to a couple of my friends at Sears. One of the girls said she had seen a Christmas tree in the dumpster that was being thrown away, so why not take that to the school? I decided to go to the store manager. I told him about the school situation and asked permission to have the discarded tree. He said absolutely not, employees are not allowed to take anything for personal use from the dumpsters. He said, "But come with me." I followed him to the department that displayed their Christmas items. He got a small tree, lights and decorations, and took a mark down on them and gave it to me for the class.

The next day, I took the decorated tree to the school and went into the classroom and the children were so excited. Mrs. Goldstein said, "What is this?"

"It's a Hanukkah bush," I replied, and set it down on a table and plugged in the lights. Mrs. Goldstein just smiled. I suggested she teach the children about Christmas and Hanukkah and leave out the parts that mentioned religion. There's nothing religious about Santa Claus. The next day they were singing Dreidel, Dreidel and Rudolph the Red Nosed Reindeer. At Easter time, we did Peter Rabbit and eggs. That same year, at Christmas, we went to Christmas Eve Services at the Lutheran Church where we were members. It was a festive evening, everyone singing songs and there was candlelight. John seemed to really enjoy himself. After the service, on the way out, everyone was greeting each other and the Pastor was at the door shaking hands. When John, in his wheel chair, rolled up to him, the Pastor put his hand on John's head and said, "Hello there, John. So good to see you here tonight. Merry Christmas to you."

John looked up at him and smiled and said, "Merry Christmas and Happy Hanukkah." He had learned about Hanukkah from his teacher, Mrs. Goldstein, at school. Guess he wanted to cover all the bases. Pastor Volz got a chuckle out of that.

In March 1976, Dr. Mahoney did the same operation on John's right leg, and he was then put into braces on both legs. He went to summer school but the following year this special education class was moved to Larkdale Elementary School. Mrs. Goldstein was still the teacher but during the year she became pregnant and was having difficulty with this pregnancy, so she took a leave of absence. John would start having one substitute teacher after the next. The class was such a difficult one that the substitute teachers didn't stay long, a week or two at most, and not only did they not get to know the children, the children never had a chance to know the teachers. The children became uncontrollable, and John became very withdrawn. He hardly ever left his desk and very seldom walked. He was still in braces, and was at a growing period in his life, and I didn't realize that his legs were becoming more rigid and in a sitting position, rather than being straight. His walking regressed with little to no activity at school. There was no physical education or recess. I asked the gym teacher why John didn't play any games and he said that John was in a group of normal children and he couldn't keep up, so he sat and watched. I complained to everyone who would listen, and that was when I decided to try and get him into a school for the physically handicapped. That school was Seagull School. I had to have three meetings with members of the school and school board before they would release John to the new school. Mrs. Goldstein, who had finally come back to school, the guidance counselor, the principal of Larkdale School, me, and a member of the school board, attended the deciding meeting. No one wanted to let go of John because he generated so much money and he was an easy child to control, unlike most of the others in the class. They knew another child would replace him, and possibly one who was harder to handle, so they really wanted to keep John.

When the lady from the school board came in, I noticed that she had braces on her legs, presumable from Infantile Paralysis. Mrs. Goldstein had obviously not noticed this. When I was making my plea for John's change in schools, Mrs. Goldstein interrupted me saying, "I don't know why you would want John to have to go to school with those crippled children and upset him seeing them and their twisted bodies." I then told them the story about the Thalidomide baby, at Carnival day at Park School in St. Louis, and how I felt things like physical appearances didn't seem to matter to John. All of a sudden the atmosphere changed, and the lady from the school board was giving me the go ahead, and said she, too, felt John would be better placed at Seagull School. Quickly, the decision was made to transfer John to Seagull. Funny how some things work out, isn't it?

12

THE SEAGULL SCHOOL YEARS

June 1978, John started Seagull School, which was a school for the physically challenged. Children with all kinds of problems attended this school, Cerebral Palsy, Muscular Dystrophy, brain damaged, accident victims and in later years, Autism. Everyone had their own problem. John was the only student who had Down Syndrome. Many of these children had normal or close to normal intelligence, so John was with people who were a challenge to his intellect, and this worked to his advantage.

It was also at this time that he began dragging his foot and complained of being tired and having pain in the knees, ankles and feet. His walking deteriorated measurably and we went again to doctors for help. Dr. Mahoney referred us to a Dr. Perry, who was a neurologist, and in July of 1978, he examined John. Parts of his findings were:

"It is my impression that this represents Down Syndrome in addition to hypertonic diplegia, which is a form of cerebral palsy. It is my recommendation that continued therapy be obtained at the Seagull School, at the Easter Seal Clinic or at any special place would be of tremendous value. We shall see him again intermittently on an as necessary basis. Sincerely J.B. Perry, M.D."

We would not hear "Cerebral Palsy" again for several years. No one took it seriously and John would continue to be misdiagnosed. The combination of Down Syndrome and Cerebral Palsy was not a common combination and was actually very rare.

His first teacher, at Seagull, was Mrs. Sandell. He liked her immediately and did pretty well in her class. These were younger children, like John, and their problems with learning were multiplied by the fact that many of them were also physically impaired, to the extent that they were in wheel chairs. So they had several things going against them. Some of his new friends were Mark, Kim, Yung, Bobby, Cheryl, Mat, Billy, Linda, Donna, Butch, Amy, Barbara, Theresa, Gary, Yvette, Julie, Lisa and Rhonda. These were just a few. They played a good part in making his life a little happier, each in their own way.

Then he had several teachers who also played a big part in his life at Seagull. There was Mrs. Nolan and Mr. Rosenberg, who were both favorites of John. They were his dedicated teachers in the last years at Seagull. Then there was Mrs. Murray, who taught him to use a sewing machine, and he made several things in her class. Mrs. Primus, his speech teacher, encouraged him with his speaking. Mr. Fox showed him how to make nameplates by engraving letters into plastic. One of these is at his grave today, it is his name, simply.... JOHN.

There were also many of the aides who helped with the children, and John knew them all. He remembered each one's birthday, and would remind me every year that "Hey, Mom, today's ------'s birthday." Some of them I didn't even remember, but he sure did. Numbers were his thing. He always remembered my social security number, as well as that of his sister and brothers. It was handy to have him along if anyone wanted to know my number...John could tell them. I never had to memorize it for myself. One of his very special aides, one that he really had strong feelings for, was Sandra Holden. John loved to call her "sexy legs." He talked about her until the very end. She really was especially nice to him, and I hope that somehow she will know how important her presence was to these special children.

In October 1978, John started walking holding both knees and was in pain most of the time. By November, he needed a walker to walk, and his walking regressed rapidly, so by January 1979, we needed help badly. John went to Dr. Brown, a child neurologist, who put him into Hollywood Memorial Hospital for a complete work up. He had all sorts of blood work done, X-rays, CAT scan, Myelogram, etc. Dr. Brown suggested an operation, and John used a wheel chair to get around most of the time after his hospital visit.

In February, he went to Jackson Memorial Hospital in Miami, to a Dr. Ayaar, who gave him a muscle test. Nothing was really helping and we decided to have him looked at by a Chiropractor, Dr. Woods. He gave John leg exercises, heat treatments, ultra sonic sound on his knees, etc. This seemed to help, for short periods of time, but nothing permanent. Finally, in June of 1979, we took John to Umatilla, Florida, to Harry Anna Hospital, for physical therapy. Harry Anna is a hospital for crippled children and was run by the Elks Clubs of Florida. They had swimming and all sorts of therapy along with schooling. He was sent to Orlando, weekly, to a Dr. Jordan, for Psychology evaluation and help. This was a time when gas was rationed, and you could only purchase gasoline for your car by the number on your license plate. Even numbers could buy on one day, and odd numbers on the next day. This made it hard for us to visit John on the weekends, as we had to go up one day and drive back the next. It took more than a tank of gas to make the trip. To get around this, a couple of times, we borrowed a license from our neighbors, and would change our plate to make the trip home. Other times, we would drive up late on Friday and come home on Sunday.

John really hated it when we would leave him. He never said a word, but when we would change his clothes to go back to the Hospital, he would start to quietly cry. It was hard on him and hard on us. They were very good to him at Harry Anna, and it was a very special hospital, but it just wasn't home. He wasn't allowed to wear his own clothes when he was there. Special clothes were assigned to him, so he knew when he saw those clothes we were taking him back. We usually rented a hotel, and would take him there when we visited. I recall one visit; we needed to get him new shoes and also a haircut. Couldn't get both of them in the same town, so we went to Eustis for one, and Umatilla for the other. One weekend, Judy drove down from Gainesville and met us there. John always liked it when his family was around. I knew after that experience, of living away from home in an institution, that he would never be happy in any kind of home, no matter how nice it was. I made up my mind then that John would always stay at home as long as I was alive and could care for him.

In October, they called us from Harry Anna and said that we needed to come after John. He missed us so much, and was actually grieving, and he had stopped trying with his therapy and was not co-operating with any-one. We brought him back home and he re-entered Seagull School. John was now in a wheel chair most of the time.

In January 1980, we took John to Dr. Halle, his pediatrician, who sug-gested that we see a Dr. Gurvey. He put John in splints and later sent him back to Dr. Ayaar, to have the muscle tests done again along with an EMG. They were now saying that John had, what they called, C1-C2 sub-luxation, which meant that the C-1-, C-2 vertebrae were moving back and forth, and they thought possibly causing damage to his spine. Dr. Gurvey asked Dr. Morrison to assist in an operation to fuse this part of his spine, but Dr. Morrison was reluctant to do the surgery, and he suggested further evaluation.

I had been in touch with my friend, Pearl Nelson, who was so very knowledgeable, and it was she who had helped so many of us in St. Louis when we were the "M & M's." She knew of a doctor who was quite smart in the field of Down Syndrome, who practiced at the Rhode Island Child Development Center, by the name of Dr. Pueschel. We contacted him and made an appointment for John to be evaluated, to confirm or to rule out the C-1, C-2 Subluxation.

In August 1980, John and I boarded a plane for Providence, Rhode Island, and the Child Development Center, which was in the Rhode Island Hospital. A friend of my husband's who was also a C.B.I. veteran met us, and he took us first to the hotel, where I left my bag, and then on to Rhode Island Hospital. John was checked in and made comfortable, and he and I ate dinner together in the cafeteria. I met, and chatted with, other people who were there for similar problems.

John went through all sorts of tests, both mental and physical, and they came to the conclusion that he did not have the C-1, C-2 Sublaxation, as had been diagnosed, and that an operation on his spine was not necessary, and could cause more brain damage. Many people, including Physical

Therapists, Nutritionists, Psychologists, Hearing and Speech specialists, evaluated John for many things, and he was given an I.Q. evaluation. Dr. Pueschel and his co-workers put John through the wringer. When they were through, we knew him inside and out. Dr. Pueschel was particularly interested in John, as he also had a Down Syndrome son, and was involved in several studies of children with Down Syndrome, their problems, and what could be done to help them.

He was interested in parents' concerns. He investigated the children's developmental function and their needs, and how to best provide optimal stimulation and enrichment to their lives. Since these children had been labeled "Mongoloids," they had been subjected to stereotyping and prejudicial downgrading, even by people who prided themselves as non-prejudicial. This labeling kept them excluded from many helpful programs and activities. To educate the public, as well as parents, Dr. Pueschel wrote a book entitled, "Down Syndrome, Growing and Learning." Along with information on the meaning and cause of Down Syndrome, it is a guidance to further the physical, social, mental and emotional growth and development of the child with Down Syndrome, giving particular emphasis to early intervention. I have always felt this was one of the MOST important things a parent should do with their children. You cannot start too early teaching them.

John and I spent several days in Providence, he staying at the hospital, and I stayed at a hotel, just a few blocks away. The first night I left him, I caught a taxi to the hotel, which wasn't far from the hospital, but you had to cross I-95 to get there, so it wasn't safe to walk. It cost me $3.00 for the taxi, so I gave the man $5.00, which included his tip. The next morning, I called for a taxi to take me back to the hospital. When it arrived, I got in and we started out and it seemed like so much longer to get there. Then I noticed we went onto I-95 and circled around somewhat. Upon arrival, the driver said, "That will be $12.00."

Well, I almost fainted. I had no idea it would cost that much, since the night before it had only been $3.00. As I left the cab, I handed the driver $12.00 and said, "The tip I am going to give you is that you need not give people a tour of Providence to take them a couple of blocks. Last night, the ride I had from the hospital to the hotel, only cost $3.00 and unless, during the night, they added more roadways, it should have been the same distance this morning." I guess it wasn't very nice on my part but I didn't like being taken for a snook. That night, when I hailed a cab, before I got in I said, "Do you think you can take me to the Ramada Hotel without giving me a tour of Providence?" I then told him about what had happened that morning, and that the night before it was only a $3.00 ride.

He said to me, "If you say it's $3.00, it's $3.00," and with that, he flipped the mileage taker and away we went. It was only $3.00 that time, too. He found out that I was staying at the hotel, and John at the hospital, and gave me his call number so I could ask for him, and he was my driver for the rest of my stay. I had never been that far away from home by myself, and I felt even more responsibility having John, who was in a wheel chair. We were both happy to get home.

Since John's legs could no longer be straightened, it was suggested that the ligaments be cut on the back side of his knees, and in October 1980, Dr. Baxt did an extensive soft tissue release on both legs. This was done at Hollywood Memorial Hospital, in Hollywood, Florida.

While this would release his knees at the knee joint, no one had allowed for the lengthening of the veins in his legs, so the operation was not quite the success we had hoped for. John had to wear stretcher splints on his legs, night and day, and they were quite painful. His legs never ever quite stretched out like they should. They told us that John should be resting on an angle, to stretch the legs, so Al made a resting board that was on an angle, about two feet high in front, and to the floor in the back. When John watched TV or was in our family room 'resting', he would lay face-down and body-down on this board. It, supposedly, would stretch out his legs. I have my doubts if it did any good, and it was a horrible experience for John.

He was measured for the splints, which were made of stainless steel and were supposed to have hinges at the joint. I was working part time, so I usually arrived at the hospital a little after lunch. The day the splints arrived, a friend, Bernie Fleischer, was visiting John. The nurses came in and started putting John's legs into the splints. They didn't fit, so the nurses were pushing down on his legs trying to force them into the splints. As I came in, I could hear John screaming loudly, and I hurried to his room. There they were, pushing down on his legs, trying to make them fit. I asked what they were doing, and they informed me that their orders were to put these on John. When I looked at them, I could see the problem…there was no hinge at the joint. They were pieces of stainless steel that were straight, and you could plainly see, these were not going to fit John. I told them that for some reason they had the wrong splints, as his were supposed to be hinged at the joint so that there was a 'give' in the straightness of them. I finally convinced them to call the doctor before doing anything more. Sure enough, the splints had been made wrong, and had to be re-made. Bernie was just furious, because he had tried to talk to these nurses and no one would listen to him, since he was not a relative. To this day, Bernie is still angry at what happened in that hospital room that day, and he speaks of it often.

Those splints cost $1,200.00, and weren't worth anything in the long run. When I told the doctor how much they cost, he couldn't believe it. He said he would have never ordered them had he realized their cost, as they were only a trial experiment anyway. I have often wondered how many things done to John were actually experiments on the part of the medical personnel.

At Seagull, John took the bus every day and returned home by bus. He became very familiar with the driver and all the students who were on the bus. He also memorized the bus numbers of all the buses that picked up students from this school, and he knew exactly which child went on which bus. My son, Tom, tried to trick him several times, by saying one kid went on such and such a bus, but John would always correct him and tell him exactly who went on which bus.

Our neighbor, across the street, is a Fort Lauderdale policeman, and it was his job to ride a motorcycle and patrol the beach area. When John's bus would come by, and he was leaving for work at the same time, he would give them a 'police escort', sirens and all, to the end of our block and out of the neighborhood area. All the kids on the bus just loved that. If Larry wasn't there, they would ask, "Hey, John, where's your cop friend?" That was another reason John had a high regard for police, sheriffs, and paramedics. He loved them all, and he loved stories about them.

He really put the bus driver to the test, also. If she was picking up a new student, or for one reason or another went a different route than usual, she would hear from John.

He would try to tell her to make a turn here or there, because that was the route he remembered to get to the school. He was definitely a child with a need for structure, a need for routine. Nothing could be changed from the norm. If it was, you heard about it.

When speaking with other mothers with children of limited intelligence, they also noted that their child needed this same sort of routine. Many of them acted violently when the routine was changed. We learned not to tell John that something was definitely going to happen, because if it didn't happen the way he thought it should, he became very angry.

For example, when we would be going away from home for the evening, he would always ask, "What time are you coming home?" He would watch the clock, and if we weren't home when we said, he became very upset. We learned to tell him a ridiculous hour like, something maybe three or four hours from the time that we felt we might return. That way, when we got home early, he was happy. We couldn't say that we were unsure of the time or that we didn't know when we would get home he just had to have a number! That would satisfy him, even though it was just a guess on our part. You couldn't make John understand that you didn't know exactly when you would be home, so we played this little game.

A funny story comes to mind, it was in 1981 or 82, and one of our neighbor's daughters, who was a good friend of Judy's, was getting married. John was invited and we went to the reception dinner at the Kapok Tree Inn, a very swanky restaurant on the outskirts of the city. We sat at a table with other friends from the neighborhood, and John was really enjoying the evening. He loved music and there was a band playing and people dancing. Appetizers were served first with little white paper napkins, with the bride and groom's names on them, Debbie and Eugene. At some point during the evening, I said to John, "Hey John, be sure and take your napkin home as a souvenir." I think I mentioned before, you had to be careful what you say to John, as he took everything literally. The evening went well and everyone had a good time. We went home and Al was unloading John from his van, which had a lift for the wheelchair.

All of a sudden, Al said, "John, what do you have there?" It seemed that John had five very large, cloth, maroon napkins tucked behind him.

He said, "Oh, those are souvenirs. Mom told me to take them. It's O K, they're clean." John had rolled around the restaurant and picked up all the napkins where people had not come to the reception, and the spaces were vacant, with napkins neatly folded. I was so embarrassed.

When the second daughter got married, and they had the reception at the same place, I jokingly asked the parents (who knew the story by this time), if they would choose the same color decor. We didn't quite have a complete set of napkins. We still get a laugh out of that, and by the way, we still have the five maroon napkins in our hall closet. Never did complete that set. It was just another time when John took words literally. That was how he handled everything.

John went through many operations in his lifetime, each one with our hopes that he would somehow be better for having had it. Numerous doctors from General Practitioners, Psychologists, Neurologists, Orthopedists and even Chiropractors, all had their share of guessing John's problem. It always amused me when they would ask us if we were sure that John was Down Syndrome. When he was tested for school here in Florida, the Psychologist who tested John said he couldn't believe John was actually Down Syndrome. When John was having a procedure at Hollywood Memorial Hospital, Dr. Brown questioned this problem with John, even though John had so very many of the Down Syndrome symptoms, the simian crease in the palms of his hands, the thick, short neck, small ears, fingers and toes, the flatness of his face, a geographic tongue, his whole body structure screamed Down Syndrome. But his intelligence belied his symptoms. Later we found out, when going through tests in Rhode Island Child Development Center at the Hospital in Providence, John functioned much better than his actual I.Q. showed. Those doctors commented that we had probably stretched John's ability as far as it could have been stretched to coincide with his actual mental intelligence. He did not test nearly as high as he actually functioned. John could read a newspaper and understand what he read. His memory was astronomical and he had a sense of humor that stumped everyone. Dr. Brown took a sample of John's blood and sent it to a Bio-Science Laboratory in Van Nuys, California. The results were as follows:

BIO-SCIENCE LABORATORIES
7600 TYRONE AVENUE
VAN NUYS, CALIFORNIA 91405

213-989-2520, EXT. 312 or 465
OUTSIDE CALIF. 800-423-3146

MEMORIAL HOSPITAL
3501 JOHNSON ST
HOLLYWOOD FLA
33021

SOURCE NO.: 54740
BSL NO.: 93-7537
COLLECTION DATE: 1/25/79
RECEIPT DATE: 1/26/79
REPORT DATE: 2/13/79

CYTOGENETIC REPORT

Patient: WILKAT, JOHN   Ref.: BROWN

TEST REQUESTED:
☐ ROUTINE
☒ EXTENDED STUDY
☐ PHILADELPHIA

SPECIMEN TYPE:
☒ BLOOD   ☐ TISSUE
☐ BONE MARROW
☐ AMNIOTIC FLUID   ☐ OTHER _____

(Please include clinical information and specimen type with your request)

CHROMOSOME STUDIES

RESULTS:

TOTAL CELLS COUNTED: 15   DISTRIBUTION: 15 cells with 47 chromosomes
                                              _____ cells with _____ chromosomes
* DATA CODE: 47,XY,21   _____ cells with _____ chromosomes

NOTES:

Bio-Science Laboratories

GIEMSA BANDING

This test may be important in determining an inherited condition, but other factors may need thorough evaluation as well. Consultation with experts at genetic counseling centers, medical centers or at other facilities with experience in this specialty is recommended if any question exists. Names of such centers will be provided on request.

Peter S. Noce

Peter S. Noce, M.D., Ph.D.
Director

* Based on Paris Conference: Standardization in Human Cytogenetics. Birth Defects: Original Article Series, 8:7, 1971, Supplement, 11:9, 1975, The National Foundation, New York.

(See reverse side for aid to interpretation.)

Dr. Brown never charged for this very expensive procedure, and we had never had John's blood tested as we had never felt the need, we had accepted the diagnosis doctors had given us when he was born. This blood test showed proof positive that John was a Trisomy 21 Down Syndrome. This, as you can see, was an extended study, with a total of 15 cells counted. He had 47 chromosomes, and there were three of the 21st in each cell. The report date of this Cytogenetic report was 2/13/79. Dr. Brown said he couldn't believe it, until he saw the results. He gave us the report for our records.

The last operation John would go through was August 19, 1982, and was performed by Dr. Strain, again at Hollywood Memorial Hospital. John had been having trouble with his left wrist, and it finally became so bad that it looked like the hand wasn't even attached to his wrist. It was offset from the wrist, as though it was misplaced. The doctor fused the left wrist to the hand and scrapped calcium from the wrist bone, so that the hand was once again at the end of his wrist. On October 28, 1982, Dr. Strain removed the steel pins from John's left wrist, and it was recast.

It was at this time that the doctors started calling John Cerebral Palsy. They finally gave up on making John the same again, and started the regimen of trying to make John as comfortable as possible. Several things were tried, but mostly he was given medication to ease the pain. John was finding it harder and harder to sit for any length of time. He was given Baclofen, Carisoprodol, Robaxin, Darvocet, Ultram, Clorazepate, and Levoxyl, just to name a few of the meds he took at different times. In 1996, he entered the Cleveland Clinic Hospital, where Dr. Nair tried using Baclofen injections next to his spine. It was probably the last procedure that John had to endure. After that, we just tried to make him comfortable.

John also had a gift of 'seeing through' people. If for some reason John didn't like someone, that person really shouldn't be trusted. He also said what he thought and sometimes this could be a hindrance. I recall one time, for instance, when we had a visit from a Veteran friend of my husband. This man was very heavy, very over-weight. My husband was talking to him and John kept interrupting with, "Boy, you are fat. Did you know that you are really, really fat?"

Each time he would interrupt, one of us would say, "John, quiet, your dad is talking with Ken and it isn't nice to say things like that to people."

It wasn't John's nature to interrupt, but for some reason he felt compelled to let this man know that he was fat. John was quiet for a little while, but when Ken got up to leave, and remembering what we had said about it not being nice to tell a person he was fat, John said, "Ken, do you know, you really have big pants." He just had to get that out!!! We have had a laugh about that many times since then.

As I look back, the happiest times of John's life, for him, was when he was in school in St. Louis, first the preschool of Montessori and then Kindergarten and First grade. He was also very happy during his years at Seagull School. He attended Seagull from June 1978 until June 1990, when he graduated. He was nearly 22 years old at that time. There was a rule that you could attend school until you were 21, but if your birthday was after school started, you could finish out that year. We opted to have John finish out the year, which gave him almost nine months more that he could go to that school. When John reached the high school level at Seagull, we had to make a decision as to the type of diploma he would receive. There were three choices, the first was the regular diploma that normal children received, the second was a special education diploma that had certain qualifications that a person must achieve before they received this one, and the third was a diploma for just attending school a certain number of days. We chose the second one, because they told me if he didn't meet the criteria, he could always get the one for time spent in school. One of the requirements for the Special Education diploma was that he must be able to multiply and divide by three numbers. John just could not seem to master this, as hard as he might try. He had completed all the other requirements, but this math thing he couldn't seem to master. The school requested that the Board of Education let John get his Special Ed diploma if they could teach him to multiply and divide by three numbers, using a hand held adding machine. They agreed, and John came through for us, albeit it took him nearly a year to comprehend. That was nearly all that John took the last year, as he had completed all other requirements. The rest of his time during the day he spent in OJT, (on the job training). They used him in the library to alphabetize the cards in books, and he also went into the younger grades and helped with the smaller children, listening to their reading and helping with simple math. He really enjoyed helping other people.

One time, there was an outbreak of flu in the school, and many of the aides were not able to be there. It put a handicap on everyone because aides were used for all sorts of things, from bathroom procedures, to feeding and helping students who could not maneuver themselves. The aides played a very important part in the daily happenings at the school. During the flu epidemic, the lunch hours were really dragging on, because there were too many children who had to be fed, and so few to feed them. One day, jokingly, one of the aides said to John, "Why don't you go over there and feed Rhonda, John. You are already finished eating." They said he looked at them and smiled, rolled himself over to where Rhonda was sitting, and started feeding her with a spoon. From then on, John fed Rhonda every day, and it really made him feel important. They became very good friends.

According to District Procedures, every exceptional student had to be reevaluated every three years. It was time for John to have a complete psychological evaluation, so he was given numerous tests and seen by several different people, including a physiologist, the guidance counselor, the exceptional education teacher and physical and occupational therapists. We were given a copy of this evaluation; this is part of the evaluation:

"John is a seventeen-year-old youngster who lives with his parents. He gets along well with all family members and very little discipline is needed, yet when it is, privileges are taken from him. His hobbies are watching TV, swimming and practicing writing his numbers. It was noted that his only friends are those at the school. His feelings about his school are very positive and he looks forward to going each day. He also enjoys riding the school bus. John is a happy person, easy to control, yet one who can be stubborn. John has a good memory and he knows how to manipulate people to his advantage. During testing, John tended to give up easily on verbal questions, yet was more persistent on visual perception and memory tasks. When asked about his family, he included his bird and dog as family members. John was a friendly youngster who appeared to put forth effort on most tasks. The results of this evaluation are considered to be a valid estimate of his abilities. At times, John's speech was difficult to understand but he readily repeated his answers when asked to do so."

13

FIELD TRIPS

During the Seagull years, John went on many field trips. Each year there was at least one 'big' trip, and money was needed to fund this. My husband thought of an idea for a Wheel-a-thon, and we presented it to the PTA. That took hold really well, and there was quite a bit of money made. The way it worked was, individuals or companies would pledge X amount of dollars for laps a certain child would make around the park. The child had to move his or her chair around a designated area, and for each lap, a certain amount of money was given. Each child had to solicit as many companies or people as they could. My husband was in a business where he had access to many businessmen, and they all came through with their share of funds. On top of this, the person who did the most laps or who got the most funds given won a prize. Sometimes the prizes were really nice things, all donated. One year, John won the first prize, and it was a very nice tape recorder/radio. It was a large one, about 12 x 24, and had all sorts of bells and whistles on it. He was so happy to get that until one little boy won 3rd prize, which was a very small portable radio, you could almost hold in your hand. Before I knew what was happening, John had traded his prize for the little radio. I tried to stop him saying, "John you don't want to give up your nice prize that you won, now do you?" Yep, he sure did…and trade it, he did. He had no idea of the value of items, and he liked the little radio. The other boy was really happy too, as he was smart enough to know he got the best of the deal. He had a normal mentality, but he suffered from Muscular Dystrophy. That same boy used to trade lunches with John. I didn't know why John was asking for different things for his lunch, until one day I went over to the school and it was lunch time.

This boy came running down the hall saying "Stop John before he starts eating." I asked why he would want anyone to stop John from eating, and he said, "He told me he would trade lunches with me, and if I don't get there in time, he'll forget and start eating his lunch." John was one of the few students who liked the school lunches, but I always made his lunch and sent it with him. This boy got free lunches from the school, but he didn't like what they served, so he would trade with John, then he would tell John what to bring the next day. I probably never would have known if I hadn't gone to school that day.

Another year, John won a prize at the walk-a-thon, which was dinner for four at a very classy restaurant down on the beach. Then, one of his friends won tickets to McDonalds, which was for a couple of meals that they had. I saw that kid going over to John and I stepped in to hear. He was trying to get John to trade with him the McDonald tickets for the four dinners at The Top of the Surf. I said, "No, John can't do that. Everyone has to keep the prize they win." John would have loved to make that trade, as "McDonalds" was one of his favorites. I had to promise him dinner at McDonalds that night, to get him to go along with what I had said. Again, he had no idea of money values. If he liked it, it didn't matter the value, he just liked it.

The money raised at these events was used to pay the expense of the students whose parents could not afford for them to go on the field trips. Like I said, they had some very nice trips, and each child in a chair had to have a 'pusher' to go with them. Then we always had at least two others along to help out with restrooms, etc., and the school nurse usually went along on these trips, also. Some of the places they went were, Disney World (John went there two times), Cypress Gardens, Sea World, Miami Seaquarium, Ocean World in Fort Lauderdale, Busch Gardens in Tampa, and the very best was Washington, D.C. for a four day trip.

On one trip to Disney World in Orlando, two of us left the other group and went on our own, because every time we went past a restroom someone would say, "Does anyone need to use the restroom?" Then everyone would stand outside until a couple of them went inside to use the facilities, instead of letting those couples catch up to the group. I could see that we were getting nowhere fast, and seeing very little at that. We decided to meet at a certain time back at the bus, and we went our merry way. Saw a lot that day, and when we arrived at the bus and met the others, they hadn't done nearly as much as we had done. Being in wheelchairs, our children were always put on rides first, and many times we were led to another entrance so these children could be loaded onto the rides. Disney World people were always very gracious and helpful to us and made the kids feel special.

One time, when we were visiting my daughter and son-in-law, also named John, in their home near Tampa, we took a trip to Busch Gardens. Since we were from St. Louis, we felt like this was a 'hometown' attraction almost, since Anheuser Busch's home office is in St. Louis, and we had many times gone there to see the plant where they made beer and also the homestead of Gussy Busch and all the Clydesdale Horses, etc. It was a free thing in St. Louis, and they had a train that took you through the park and all the grounds, and the trip ended at the barns, where the Clydesdale Horses were stabled. So we felt like this was a good place to go. The facility, in Tampa, was altogether different however, mostly being rides. We went anyway and it wasn't free, like St. Louis, but that was O K, too. I went over to one of the rides that were like little swings that went around in a circle. The ride wasn't filled and no one was waiting to ride, so I started to put John on the ride. The person in charge said, "He can't go on that if he can't walk."

I said, "Well, he doesn't have to walk to sit in the seat."

He said, "That doesn't matter, he can't go on the rides if he can't walk."

I said, "I'll be glad to lift him onto the seat."

He said, "No, if he can't walk, he can't ride."

Now I was getting a little ticked off so I said, "You know, when we went to Disney World, they were very nice, and not only did they let him ride any ride he wanted, they actually lifted him on the ride themselves."

He said, "Lady, this isn't Disney World. If you can't walk, you can't ride."

I then told him that at no point had anyone told us that he would not be allowed to ride and they certainly took our money, just like they did everyone else, when we came in, and that I intended to write Gussy Busch and tell him what I thought about the rules they were using in their Tampa Park. I never did write to Mr. Busch, but now that I think about it, I really should have.

Things have surely changed by now. More people are conscious of handicapped persons, and consideration is being made more freely. At the time, I was very upset, and I still have bad feelings about Busch Gardens. Disney World gives me only warm feelings, their personnel really bent over backwards to make us feel wanted and show us a good time.

One of the trips that was an overnight trip, we went first to Sea World, and the next day, drove to Cypress Gardens. My daughter and son-in-law to be went to school in Gainesville, and they met us at Cypress Gardens, to help with pushing the kids. The first day, I was in charge of three boys, one being John. The other two were Kelly and Butch. Kelly was in a wheelchair, but Butch was Autistic, and he could walk, so he pushed Kelly and I pushed John. There were quite a few pretty steep slopes and I had to watch that Butch didn't push Kelly off the path. We had lots of laughs that day. Kelly had Cerebral Palsy and he was actually a pretty smart kid. That night we shared a room in the motel and John and Kelly wanted to watch TV. Butch didn't want to watch, so he took his shower first. The bath had fixtures that were a little complicated, the hot and cold water came from the same spigot, and you had to adjust the temperature with a lever, so I went in before him and got the water a pleasant temperature. He took his pajamas into the bathroom with him and was there for quite awhile. Then, when he came out, I really wasn't paying much attention but was watching the TV when Kelly said, "Butch, what are you doing? Mrs. Wilkat is right here." With this, I turned to see Butch taking off his pajamas and looking for underwear to put on under the pajamas. This was the way he had learned, and like John, he didn't like change. I went into the bathroom to get it ready for Kelly and, to my surprise there wasn't a drop of water anywhere, on the floor, in the sink or in the tub. Butch had dried every inch of that bathroom with a towel before he left it.

The next day, Judy and her boyfriend met us at Cypress Gardens. It was a good thing too, as there was one hill after another, and I really don't think I could have maneuvered two wheelchairs there. We were going to one of the attractions when Judy's friend came over and said do you think Judy and I could change who we are taking care of? They made the change, Judy took over with Butch and her friend pushed Kelly. Later, we found out that Butch wanted to hold hands with whoever was with him. Butch was almost 6 ft. tall, and the boy was embarrassed at holding hands with someone who looked very normal. Judy didn't mind though, and we all had a good time. The only trouble was, Butch had a schedule and we had to see everything as it was listed on the schedule, no matter what side of the park it was on. Also, Judy is only a little over 5 ft. tall and she had to take two or three steps to every one that he took. Whenever we finished looking at one attraction, Butch would say, "The next event is…" whatever was listed next, and we would have to hurry there to make it on time. It was an experience for all of us, and my daughter's friend learned what it was like to have a handicapped brother, like Judy had. Later, the two of them married and he fit right into our family and was always as helpful with John as if he were his very own blood brother. Our John really loved the new John.

John with his sister, Judy
and Brother-in-law, John Stoner

14

THE WASHINGTON D.C. TRIP

You had to know John to understand how much this particular trip meant to him. He was always interested in our President and our past Presidents and has several books and videotapes about them and their lives, along with videos about the First Ladies. He just couldn't get enough of learning and hearing about different Presidents. His very favorite, I think, was possibly John F. Kennedy. I don't know if it was his name or something else that John related to, but President Kennedy was definitely one of John's heroes. Now we were going to the city where these famous people were living or had once lived. He was very excited.

This trip was probably the most fun of all the trips we had ever taken. We had never before been gone for more than one night on any of our field trips. This trip would take us to a place none of us had seen and we would be gone for four days. As I recall, we left on a Monday morning and would return home on Friday. We were there Monday night, Tuesday night, Wednesday night and Thursday night, and early Friday morning we came back home. We stayed at a Holiday Inn, where the parking was under the motel and was actually the first floor. Two buses had been rented to carry all of us, one with a lift for the wheelchairs, and the other was just a regular bus that the 'pushers' rode in. As you can see, there was quite a crowd, 18 wheelchairs and two "walk on's" (these were children who could walk but had some other kind of handicap.) Then, with their pushers, the extra pushers, a teacher or two and the nurse, we had quite a crowd. It was a job just getting everyone on the plane, as each child had to go aboard in their chair up to the door, then they were transferred to a small rolling platform the airlines use, and they were rolled to their seat. A blanket was placed under them on their seat, in case we had to evacuate in a hurry, it was easier to grab the four corners of the blanket and hoist that child out of the seat. Then, that wheelchair was removed and placed with the luggage inside the plane, and another child was boarded. As you can imagine, it took awhile to load and unload us, but we made it. Patience is the KEY word when you are working with handicapped people.

After John and I were loaded in the plane, a stewardess came to me and said, "If we have to evacuate for any reason, you stay seated by your son and someone will come and help you."

I told her, "If this plane goes down, I will be crawling over all these people with him on my back. Don't think I am waiting until someone gets around to helping me." She just laughed. We had lunch on the plane, and then landed in Washington D.C.

We were met at the plane by our buses and taken to the hotel to check in. Then, we boarded the buses again and were taken to the underground train station called the Metro Subway, which was very close to our Hotel. We had our first meal there and the kids were really having a good time. They got to choose their dinner from several items, as it was a cafeteria setting. What fun they did have. You would never know that they had made a plane trip from Ft. Lauderdale and just how tired they really were. So many of these kids lived in group homes, and either didn't have parents or didn't live with them. I guess most of them probably had never been that far away from home before. Most of the pushers were aides from the school, but there were several teachers and a couple of other youngsters who had come from another high school in Fort Lauderdale, Chaminade Madonna. They had volunteered their time to take care of another kid and be their legs and arms, for the four days. We always took the school nurse on these trips, nurse Nancy, and this time there was a couple of other women who volunteered. We were placed in rooms of four people to a room. John and I shared a room with two of the women. One was the mother of an aide at the school. These kids were making memories that would stay with them the rest of their lives.

After dinner that first night, we were loaded into the buses and taken for a night view of all the monuments that are in Washington D.C. It was just beautiful seeing them illuminated in the night, and as we drove around, the driver was giving a documentary of each place saying, "Over on the left side you will see the Washington Monument." Then, a little later, "Over to your right is Lincoln's Memorial," and she would tell a little about that one. But several times she pointed out "Washington's Monument," as it seemed to loom up on first one side and then the other. After a couple of times of this, John piped up and said, "You already showed us that one before, lady." Everyone had a good laugh over this. I guess he thought she was confused about where she was.

Ever after that, no matter where we were, if anyone saw the Washington Monument they would yell, "Hey, John, there's the Washington Monument."

He would always reply, "Very funny, ha. ha."

Our time was limited with so much to see, and loading and unloading wheelchairs took a lot of time, but we went from early morning until 8 or 9 P.M. each day and, although they were really pooped little kids, they took it in stride and no one complained.

Our morning always started with a cafeteria-style breakfast at the hotel, and we were usually on our way by 9:00 or 9:30. One day, we went over to Virginia and Monticello, where Thomas Jefferson lived. It is located 125 miles from Washington, D.C. We went all through that beautiful place and the grounds. Even the ride back to the hotel, taking the same road that Jefferson took to Washington, made quite an impression on the kids. We saw the fields that he had planted many years ago, but I think what made the most impression on them was the back of Monticello, which is also on our nickel. We showed them the back of the nickel and then they saw the place itself...unbelievable to them. They were in awe.

Another day, we went to the U.S. Mint and watched them make money. All the kids said they wanted 'samples'. They really got a kick out of seeing money being made and printed right before their very eyes. We had lunch at the Old Post Office and that was a thrill. Then, we went to the Capitol Building and the White House. Our picture was taken on the steps of the Capitol, and Representative Clay Shaw met with us there and he was included in the picture. Later, he sent each of us a copy of the picture and signed each picture. There are 43 people in the picture, including Clay Shaw. John was in the front, with Representative Shaw behind him. The Capitol looms behind us. John was always very proud of that picture. He had met Clay Shaw before in Ft. Lauderdale when he went to Representative Shaw's office to have his picture made. The same day he went to the office of Mayor John Lomelo, in Sunrise, Florida, and had pictures taken for some kind of promotional thing they were having.

We also went to the White House, but only saw a small portion there, as the President was inside, so visitors were limited. Then, another day, we went to Arlington Cemetery and saw the graves of John F. Kennedy and his son, along with that of his brother, Robert Kennedy. We were told the story that at one point along the way, Robert Kennedy had come to the cemetery and looking out over the vast beautiful grounds, he made the remark that he could live here forever. Little did he know that that was where his remains would spend eternity!

There are lots of hills in the cemetery and pushing wheelchairs wasn't easy, but it was well worth it. It was a memorable experience for us all.

Another place that John remembered so well was Mount Vernon. Lots of hills here, too, but the children were very interested in the tour and hearing about our President, George Washington. This was his home. John said, "He was my second father. He was the father of my country." I always thought that was a strange way of looking at it, but that was what was seen through the eyes of John. They all thought it funny that George Washington has false teeth made out of wood.

On one occasion, we were to eat at a restaurant in Virginia. It was 5 o'clock traffic, and we were following the bus with the children down Pennsylvania Avenue. After coming to a stop, our bus stalled and the driver could not get it started, try as she might. They called for assistance from the lady who had booked this whole tour for us and she phoned for several taxis to come and pick us up. In the mean time, the first bus with all the kids was trekking on down the road to Virginia, unaware that we were not following. The taxis finally arrived, but it took a while with such heavy traffic. We were all loaded into the cabs, four to a cab, and away we went. Our driver didn't speak English, and didn't know where he was going. He was told to follow one of the others. Here we were, going 90 miles an hour it seemed, down the highway, in and out of traffic as he tried to keep up with the guy in front. At one point, we went flying by a police car, and I had visions of being in a jail cell, calling my husband in Florida, to tell him I had no earthly idea of where John was at that moment. We made it to our destination and had dinner and then went back to the hotel, and was I ever glad to see that Holiday Inn.

As we pulled in under the hotel (the parking was under the hotel), the kids had already started being unloaded. All of a sudden, someone under there blew their car horn. Being under the hotel, it magnified the sound, and it was very loud. It startled Mat, who was one of the 'walk on's', and he grabbed a newspaper rack that was there and threw it as hard as he could, and he ran and jumped on an elevator before anyone could stop him. Now, we had aides running as hard as they could to get on other elevators, to try and catch him. We didn't know if he would know which floor to get off on, so they were stopping at each floor. Sure enough, Mat, like John, never forgot anything. He was waiting in front of the door to his room, which was on about the 8th floor.

Another incident that comes to mind as I write this is, one evening we were having dinner and across the table from John and I was a young man from Chaminade High School, who had been taking care of a little black boy who was severely handicapped. This little boy drooled constantly and when he was fed, the food would run out of his mouth and had to be scraped back in several times. It wasn't a pleasant sight, but as a mother I could understand. I noticed that this young man was feeding the little boy first, and hadn't touched his own food. I mentioned that perhaps he could take a few bites and then give his ward a bite or two, before his food got cold.

He said "No, I know he's really tired and I want to get as much food into him as I can. If I stop, he wants to quit eating, so I'll eat after he is finished." I offered to help him and he politely turned me down saying he had volunteered to do this, and he would do it. During our conversation, I found out that he had been accepted to West Point the following year. He was very proud of that. He started telling me how things would be at West Point. He said he knew the first year was the hardest, as the older cadets would try and make the newcomers feel like they were useless.

My heart just broke, to think that anyone could think that this young man was useless. I said "Listen here, the first time someone tries to make you feel like "a nobody" or that you are useless, you remember this night, and you know in your heart that they could not do what you are doing at this moment. You are far from useless, and don't you ever forget it. You have given this child, who is nothing to you, a moment in his life that no one else would or could give him. You are far from useless, and don't you ever let anyone try to put you down." This memory has stayed with me all these years, and I often wondered what happened to that wonderful young man.

While we were there, we went to the Smithsonian but first we went to the National Museum of Natural History where we saw all sorts of animals that had been stuffed. Then we made our way over to the National Air and Space Museum. Each child was allowed to purchase one item, as a souvenir. John rolled around and around, looking at first one thing and then another. He finally decided on a mobile made up of airplanes. I tried to talk him into something else that he could hold, but he would have nothing else. We brought it home and it hangs, to this day, from the ceiling in his room, near the foot of his bed. I guess he was smarter than I was. He enjoyed looking at that for the rest of his years, and each time the heat or A.C. came on, there was just enough air to start the little planes flying, tipping their wings, as if to wave a hello to John.

Our trip to Washington was a very memorable one, and we talked about it often. I don't know if they ever took another trip that lasted as long or was as much fun, but not while John attended Seagull.

John always had a smile on his face.
Way to go, John!

15

PROMS

They weren't known as Senior Proms, just the Prom. That was because there usually weren't many seniors at one time, so everyone who was a teenager was invited. Prom was something that all the kids looked forward to and it usually was during the month of May. Each year there was a 'theme' for the prom and usually there were a couple of souvenirs with the theme printed on them.

The first year John went to the prom was in 1984, and the theme that year was "Puttin' on the Ritz." He still has the little candle in a glass container with that written on the side. The school colors were blue and white, so that theme was also carried out. It was usually held at Rolling Hills Country Club, at least the last few years that's where they had it. There was a dinner, followed by music and dancing. If you might wonder how they could dance in wheelchairs, vision two people, each in a wheelchair, holding hands and moving their chair from one side to the other, in time to the music. It was a sight to behold. The aides from the school usually attended and they would 'dance' with the students, too. One musical group, called Ted Vernon and the Bull Dogs, took an interest in the school and kids, and they played for them several years. A couple of the songs they sang were, "Jail House Rock", "I Feel Good" and "Do Love." All the music was sort of Rock and Roll and it all had a jazzy beat. Each year a couple was voted to be Prom Queen and King. In 1987, a pretty young girl named Julie C. was the queen and Gary Mc. was the king. That was a fun year and stands out in my memory as one of the best, maybe because that was the year we went to Washington for our field trip.

One year, John ended up with 2 dates. Another mother and I had arranged for her daughter and John to go to the Prom. This young girl's name was Dawn. She was a very pretty girl but was confined to a wheel-chair by Spina Bifida. He went to several of the proms with Dawn and they got along well with each other. At school, another girl asked John to take her to the prom. I felt sorry for her, as she didn't have parents, but I couldn't back out on the other girl either. The teachers got the two girls together and they agreed that John would take both girls. That year, we had to buy two corsages and John sat between the two girls at the dinner. He really enjoyed himself as he said, "With two girl friends." Since most of the kids had to be transported by a van, when you had a date, you met her at the dance. Al and I usually volunteered to be chaperones, and we would attend and have dinner with the group of teachers and aides. Al would take videotapes of the affairs and then we would transfer them to tapes for our television. If John asked you if you wanted to see his prom tape, unless you had a couple of days to watch TV, your answer should be, "No, thank you." The tape we have has about four years of proms on it and lasts about 6 hours, that's a whole lot of proms.

John's prom year was 1990, May 4th. The theme that year was "NEVER SAY GOOD-BYE." What an appropriate sentiment. It was John's theme for life, and now it will be mine. It was etched on a glass that was the souvenir that year. John got two of them and they are on a shelf in his room. He really thought he was hot stuff that night and he did look handsome. It was held at Rolling Hills Country Club. Even though he was invited to the Prom several years after he graduated, he didn't ever want to go back. He would say, "No, that's O K. I had my Prom." He did enjoy 'his prom' very much and the tape has almost worn out, he watched it so many times.

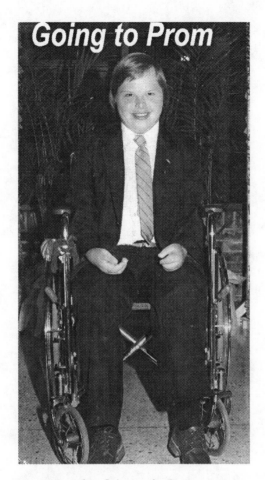

John, Going to the Prom

16

OTHER MEMORIES OF SEAGULL

John was always impressed with anyone of importance, and he also was very interested in politics. He always voted, using the absent tee ballot, but he always voted.

One of his favorite people was the Broward Sheriff Officer, Nick Navarro. John referred to him as Sheriff Nick. John would call himself, 'Sheriff John'. One time when John was going to Seagull, the Sheriff's office sent Nick Navarro to the school for goodwill purposes, I suppose. He arrived via helicopter and the all the kids were outside to watch the plane land on the lawn. The Sheriff handed out pens and talked to the kids about safety. After the speech, John rolled over to him and said, "I voted for you, you know. So did my mom and dad." Sheriff Navarro thanked him for his vote and said he hoped John would vote for him the next time he ran for office. John assured him that he would definitely be voting for him.

When election time rolled around I just hated it…John wanted to listen to every speech that anyone made. In one of the elections, after we had heard one person after another and we were all getting pretty tired of the rhetoric, John was insisting on listening to Dan Quayle. I said, "Come on John. You don't care what he is talking about. Let's get something else on TV."

"No," he said, "He's talking about me."

I said, "No, he's not, John, what makes you say that?"

He was indignant. "YES, HE IS. HE'S TALKING ABOUT THE YOUTH OF OUR COUNTRY, AND THAT'S ME."

I had to hold on to keep from laughing. He was right. As I listened, that is exactly what Dan Quayle was talking about, and again he was right, as he was the 'youth of our country'. He knew more than I did about what was going on!! You'd think I would learn. John didn't talk much, but you could usually put money on what he did say.

He really got very interested when there was an election. He always wanted to read the papers about what was being said about one person or another. If you had a different opinion from John, forget it. You could not change his mind. One time, I recall, Pat DeLong, a friend of ours, tried to convince John that the Democrat person running for some office was the best one to vote for. John was adamant...he was voting for the other person. He wasn't for a Republican or Democrat, he didn't care about one party or another, just the person and what they stood for. Nothing could dissuade him from his decision. He was like that!!!

After he had voted, he always wanted the little sign that says "I Voted" put up in his room. He was proud of his vote, and wanted everyone to see that. How may other people do you know are actually proud that they voted?

If John liked something, he gave it 120%. There was no doing something just a little bit. For example, he liked the St. Louis Cardinals baseball team. He just wouldn't miss a game they were playing. He never went to a game when we were in St. Louis, but he felt a tie to that team. A friend of ours, Susan Brown, used to send him all sorts of things with St. Louis Cardinals on it, and he had those things on his walls, his dresser, and his chairs, everywhere. Susan used to send him e-mails, too, and I would print them out for him to keep. He had those emails stuffed everywhere. John was a pack rat for sure. He also saved different cards, birthday cards, Christmas cards, any holiday card he would get he saved. Susan never let a holiday go by without sending him a card for that day, and he had saved them all. Sometimes he would let me throw away cards from others after they became worn, but not the ones from Susan. They didn't know each other in St. Louis, but after we moved here, she came to visit her parents who were friends of ours, and she became fond of John and sort of took him under her wing.

At Christmas, John only seemed interested in what Susan had sent to him. All the rest was 'second fiddle' to Susan's gifts. She usually sent several things, each wrapped individually in a large box, so it took awhile to go through all the gifts she sent to him. How happy he was then...I often wonder if she had any idea just how happy she had made his life with her remembrances...I don't think so.

With other cards he received, he would sometimes give them to other people who were having a birthday. It didn't seem to matter that someone else signed the card; he just wanted to give that person a card. Sometimes if Al or I would go away for a day or so, he would always give us something, some little trinket, to take with us. When we returned, he would expect us to have something for him from our trip. It could just be a bar of soap from the hotel. He really didn't care, just so you brought him something.

One time, I think it was last year, my granddaughter was having a birthday. Her family came over and we were having a little celebration. Her birthday is April 5th and her brother's birthday is April 15th so they are celebrated close together. On Ally's birthday, John called her into his bedroom. At this time he wasn't really able to sit for long periods of time, so he spent most of his time in his room in his bed, which was adjustable and more comfortable for him. She came over to his bed and he said, "Happy Birthday, Sweetheart." Then he reached behind his head to the shelf on his bed and got his little wallet, where he kept money that different people had given to him. He reached inside, handed her a $10.00 bill and said, "This is for you." She didn't want to take his money and tried to turn it down. We told her, if John wants you to have it, it is his to give away, and if that makes him happy, please take it. So she did, and later she wrote him a very nice note thanking him for it.

April 15th rolled around, and again the family got together for a celebration of A.J.'s birthday. He was several years younger than his sister. He walked in and out of John's room...nothing. Then he went in and said, "Hey, John, did you know today's my birthday?"

John said, "Yep, Happy Birthday little buddy," and that was it.

Well, A.J. was perplexed, so he said, "John, you got anything you want to give me?"

John fumbled around and got a 'used card' that said happy birthday, and handed it to A.J. John said, "Here you go."

Not to be let down, A.J. said, "John, you gave Ally some money, don't you remember? Don't you want to give me some money?"

John said, "O K", and then he reached behind his head, got his little wallet, reached inside and pulled out a bill and handed it to A.J.

A.J. looked at it and said, "John, this is just a ONE dollar bill. You gave Ally TEN." His mother hurried him out of the room and tried to tell him that to John, one bill was like the next. John really had no concept of money or of its value.

One time when he was in the hospital my mother used to send him a card every day. In the card she would always put a dollar bill. He was always glad to get her card.

On one of the days when she was sending a card, she didn't have any dollars to put inside, but she had been to the cafeteria, which was having an opening, and they had given everyone balloons with their logo on them. My mother enclosed the deflated balloon in her card and sent that. When John got that card he was so excited, "Bal Loones" he said, "Bal Loones." After that, I told my mom how excited he was over the balloon, so every time she sent a card from then on, it had a balloon inside and he really looked forward to getting her cards.

After we moved to Florida, John was bounced around from one school to another. There didn't seem to be any set place for these kids to attend school. One year they would go to one school, and the next to another school. It was very trying on the children and as a result, the parents didn't take part in the school activities like they might have. The first school John attended was Pine Ridge Elementary School, with Mrs. Smith as his teacher. The following year he was assigned to Plantation Elementary School, and his teacher was Mrs. Goldstein. The third year he was assigned to Larkdale Elementary School and Mrs. Goldstein was his teacher again, but she took a leave of absence to have a baby and was out most of that year. They had one substitute after another, none of them lasting more than a couple of weeks, if that long. All of this took it's toll on John, and his walking became more labored, to the point that he was using a walker part time and was very tired most of the time. We didn't realize how this was affecting him emotionally. It was at this point that I looked into alternative schooling and found Seagull School, which was a school that took different disabilities, but was mainly for the physically handicapped. Other disabilities included Muscular Dystrophy, Autism, Spiny Bifida, Cerebral Palsy, and accident victims (one girl had been hit by an automobile and was left both with physical and mental handicaps, and another was a victim of gas escaping from a heater and almost asphyxiated her and her family. She was the worst hit from this, and it left her with both physical and mental handicaps.) Later, they also had classes for girls who were pregnant and didn't want to attend their regular school. It seemed to be a 'catch all' school, because everyone had their own problem. This was good in many ways. Each child could respect the other, because they understood what it was like to be different. Many of the children were slow mentally, but others were very smart, so your mentality didn't seem to matter. You worked at your own speed, and since everyone had some kind of handicap, no one made fun of the others.

I had a difficult time getting the school board to change John's schooling, but as I wrote before about this problem, I did finally get him into Seagull.

The school was also a great place for John, since they offered both physical therapy and speech therapy. He would not get this in a 'normal' school, at least not as much as he did at Seagull. In this state, the money for children in schools goes to the placement of the child. It is also regulated by that child's disability. The school that John attended got money first, because he went there, secondly, because he was physically handicapped and then more money because of his mental handicap. He needed two kinds of therapy and they received money for this. When he first started at Seagull, the children were taken across the street to the Easter Seal Clinic's building. The state paid money for the therapy children received from this Clinic. A couple of years later, it was brought up in a PTA meeting, that perhaps instead of giving that money to the Easter Seal

Clinic, we could hire full time therapists for the school. After looking into this, that was what they did. They hired both physical and occupational therapists, and they were on campus all the time. It was a win-win situation. Our kids got therapy every day.

The school board was always looking for ways to 'cut the budget', and our school was taking a big chunk of change from their budget. Someone on the board got the idea to close down Seagull and send the kids back to individual schools with classrooms in the regular schools. They were also suggesting that we integrate our children into the regular classes, saying it would be so much better if they were around normal children. This would eliminate quite a few teacher salaries, and the expense of keeping a school open. They made it sound like a really great idea for everyone. A parents meeting was called for one evening, and a lady from the school board was coming to tell all the parents how wonderful this was going to be for their children.

So many of these kids lived in group homes already, and their parents either didn't care, or were not aware of what was happening. So many of them never ever heard from their parents anyway. They were at the mercy of those of us who really cared.

I went to the meeting and sat in disbelief at what I was hearing, and how those parents who were attending the meeting were reacting to this. The school board lady began telling how our children would be taken into regular classes, and how they could have normal friends, etc. etc. They would be sending therapists to the different schools, periodically, to give therapy to those who might need it. She didn't bother to tell them that not only would this cause a hardship on the therapists who would be traveling from school to school, each school could not have the equipment needed for their use. Then, too, they couldn't be at every school every day, so it would probably be on a weekly basis (if we were lucky). Obviously, no one on the school board was aware of or cared that most of these kids needed therapy every day, and as often as possible, just to keep them going.

I sat and listened to this pretty speech. I watched as the other parents nodded in agreement to what was being said. At the end of her talk, she asked if there were any questions. I had to raise my hand, and as I was the only one with a question, she called on me. I said, "Do you have any children who are school age?"

"Why, yes I do," she said.

I said, "Before you take our children out of this special school and an environment that they are used to, and that they enjoy, I ask that you, and the other school board members, visit a hatchery where they hatch out those darling little chickens. Just watch, as those cute little chicks peck to death the little chick who isn't well or who isn't just right. That is the way your darling little children will peck at our children, if you put them into this atmosphere. They will do either one of two things as I have seen it happen with my own eyes. There will be your children who will make fun of ours and taunt them. Then there will be the others, who will feel sorry for them and try to do everything for them, taking away their independence. Our children are encouraged to do for themselves when they can, and they don't need to have this taken away from them. I think everyone here will agree that they don't want their child made fun of, or being the brunt of the jokes. Our kids need their therapy every day, not just whenever someone happens to come by. I think the school board should take a long hard look at this, before they make this very important decision. If there are parents who want their children put into normal schools, then let them go, but as for me, I want my son to continue in this school that he has come to love."

The meeting was over, and we never heard another word from the school board about changing the school.

17

GRADUATION

John was chosen 'Best of the Class', and he appeared on television station WBPS-TV, as Best of the Class 1990, Seagull School. Each high school in Broward County had someone who was picked the best, and one student from each school was on television, each on a different day. We asked for a video copy of the program that contained John, and they were kind enough to send us one.

Seagull didn't have many children attending, and the school went from First grade through 12th grade, or High School. Some years, there were more people graduating than others. For example, in 1986 there were eight students who graduated, in 1988 there were six students, but the year John graduated 1990, there were only two graduates. The other boy lived in a group home, and they didn't even bring him to the graduation, and John was alone that graduation day. No matter, all the school and staff treated it as though there were hundreds of students graduating. John wore a cap and gown and speeches were given and Pomp and Circumstance was played. It was just like a big ceremony.

Mr. Rosenberg, his teacher, pushed John up the ramp onto the stage. There he was, so proud of himself. It was his big night, and he was enjoying every minute of it.

The smile on his face was priceless, and there he sat, on stage, all alone like most of his life, but he was in his glory. Ever so often he would slightly make a wave with his hand, as it rested on the arm of his wheel chair, and there was the big grin, saying, here I am, I made it.

His Principal gave a speech, telling how John had come to their school and all the things he had participated in, including our field trips. Then, a couple of teachers and aides spoke, each telling of their experiences with

John. One recalled he always called her sweetheart, O K, sweetheart, etc. If he liked you, and you were female, you were called sweetheart. For the guys, they were called buddy.

John was valedictorian, and he gave a speech, which we were very proud to hear. We had no part in his writing the speech, but he did get help from some of the teachers.

I couldn't believe that he could be in front of so many people and make that speech. How very proud we all were of him that day. He was the first Down Syndrome person to receive a special education diploma in the county, possibly in the whole state of Florida.

Members of the school board always presented diplomas to the graduates of each school, and there was a lady from the school board, by the name of Dianne Wasserman, who was there to present John with his diploma. She gave a speech, and in it said, "John, I will be giving out hundreds of diplomas this year, at different schools, but this diploma I am giving to you tonight means more to me that all the others combined, as I know that you probably worked harder to get this than anyone else that will receive one."

There was quite a crowd that night, people coming from all around, our friends, relatives and nearly every one of the staff, including teachers and aides. There was a representative from the Broward County Sheriff's office, who presented John with a savings bond. Several members of the therapy team were there, along with numerous people who had an interest in Seagull School. We made a videotape of the whole graduation, and John looked at it often, remembering the night that he had worked so hard to make happen.

There were refreshments for all who came, a big sheet cake with his name on it and punch. And that was the final day for John at Seagull School—a place that he kept in his heart all his days.

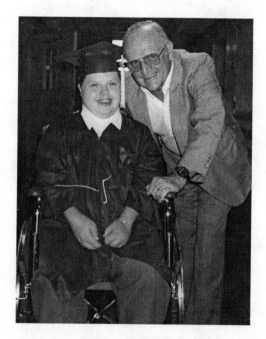

John with his Dad, graduation night

John with nephew, A.J. Stoner

18

AFTER GRADUATION

After graduation day, nothing was quite the same for John in the way of schools. He was never really happy any place that we found for him. One day, I found him in his room and glanced into his trashcan. I was shocked to find he had taken his diploma down from the shelf where it was kept. He was trying to tear it up. I could hardly believe it. I asked him why he would do such a thing, and he told me, "I don't want to be graduated. I hate that. I want to go back to Seagull School." I guess he thought if that diploma didn't exist, he would be able to go back to the Seagull School he loved so much.

I tried to explain to him that throwing away the diploma, which he worked so hard to get, would not undo his graduation. He still would be a graduate from Seagull and he could not go back. In John's thinking, if he just got rid of that diploma, it would change things. He would be a student again in the school he so dearly loved, with people who were his friends for so many years and with teachers who treated him with the respect he so deserved.

Since John's passing I have thought on this several times. I cannot tell you how much I would like to "throw away that death certificate," and turn back the clock to a yesterday. Wouldn't it be wonderful, if we could just go back to another time, to undo all the things that went wrong in our life? The computers these days sure have it on us. Now, if you have Windows XP on your computer, and you make a mistake, you just go back a day, a week or to whenever it was better. Then you start again. How great it would be to have our lives in the Windows XP mode, and when our life crashes, we would just go back and make changes and relive the yesterdays of our lives. Unfortunately, life is not in the Windows XP mode, we are still in Windows 98 mode, and when life crashes, life crashes. There's no going back to what could have been. We just have to go ahead with what is left and make the best of that.

We found a couple of adult education classes where John went, but none of them compared to Seagull and what he got there. At one, the teacher, Florence, was a lovely woman, and she truly liked John, but the other students attending were not nearly as advanced as John. Most of them had been in 'trainable' classes, and now they were learning the A, B, and C's. John was very bored. I recall, one day they told me that the following week they were going to start teaching John how to tell time. I said, "You've got to be kidding. John could tell time when he was in second grade." It seems that he was so angry that someone would try and teach him something like that he played "dumb," and pretended that he didn't know how to tell time. He did the same thing when it came to writing. One day he told me, those people are stupid.

We had to drive John to school and pick him up. It hardly seemed worth it, as he went from 9:00 A.M. to 2:00 P.M. We hardly got home until it was time to go pick him up, but it did give him somewhere to go. John was having a harder time making himself understood, also. His tongue seemed to be larger and it was harder and harder for him to pronounce words. Many times he became frustrated and would say, "Forget it!" Then, if you encouraged him more, he would spell what he was trying to say. Imagine yourself, trying to say words, knowing exactly what you want to say and not being able to make your mouth do what you want to make the words so others could understand. I think that this is probably how stroke patients must feel. It was very frustrating for John.

One day, I was driving John to school and a big very fat Muskogee duck tried to fly in front of our van, but being too fat, it couldn't get up high enough to clear the van. POW! We hit the duck and it went flying over the top of the van and into the street behind us. I was so worried that this was going to upset John. When he was younger, and first going to school, there used to be a flock of ducks that he would feed bread to every day when he got home from school. It became such a tradition that the ducks used to wait for his school bus, and when it came around the corner, here came the ducks running as hard as they could after the bus so they could get their treat. As soon as he was off the school bus, I gave him the bread and he would throw it to his feathered friends. He got such a thrill doing this and he looked forward to it as much as the ducks did. After we hit the duck, I didn't know how to handle it so he wouldn't be upset. When I got John unloaded from the van at school, I took the teacher aside and told her what happened and how John considered the ducks his friend. I said if he should start crying or anything, to give me a call but I wanted them to know of the traumatic incident so they could watch for any unusual behavior in John. I went home and worried all morning about him. I decided to make something special for his dinner that evening, something he really liked. Then I went to the school to pick him up. His teacher said there was nothing unusual and John was just fine as far as she could tell.

While driving home, I was playing music that he liked on the radio. I said to him, "John, mom is making you something very special for supper tonight. Can you guess what it is?"

Just that quick John replied, "No, but I sure hope it's not duck." Seeing things through John's eyes...

This adult program didn't seem to be the right program for John, so we started looking around for an alternative situation. That's when we enrolled him in the ARC Program. Actually I think they refer to it as the BARC program, which stands for Broward Association for Retarded Citizens. Their program had a workshop where the clients (as they were called) could do certain things and they would get paid for it. Companies would have them counting screws, or something like that, and put them into a little bag. You were paid for the number of bags you had made. Checks came every two weeks. John never made much. I think the worst paycheck was 32 cents. That was his last one, they mailed it to him, paying 37 cents postage and no telling how much to process the check. If that wasn't bad enough, they sent it via return receipt request, which I don't remember how much more that cost them.

I was called in for an interview with the counselor and John. She kept talking to him about working harder, he said, "No, that's O K."

Then she said, "If you make money you can go to the store and buy things you want."

He said, "No, that's O K."

Then she said, "John, wouldn't you like to make money and go to the mall, and you could buy whatever you wanted for yourself?"

John said, "No, that's O K, my dad will get it for me." He knew his dad well.

She said it was really a shame that he wouldn't work because he was one of the very few students they had that could actually count the right number of articles to be placed in the bags. He just was bored and he refused to do it. I really can't say I blame him. It was almost insulting to him.

They put him in another section where, again, they were teaching far below his level and he just hated it. He didn't want to go to the school, and he was getting very upset when we would take him. He started going to the bathroom in his pants so they would call me to come get him. We finally took him out altogether and decided that he was better off staying at home. He was getting much harder to move about, as he had put on a great deal of weight. He didn't want to go to that place and nothing else was available.

A month later, I was called on the phone for an interview. It seems that this is the procedure when someone withdraws from the ARC program. During the conversation, the lady said, "I certainly hope John's leaving wasn't because of Billy biting people. Most of the clients could get away from him, but John, being in the wheelchair, made it hard for him to get away from him."

I couldn't believe what I was hearing. John had never complained about someone biting him, he just said the people there were crazy. I told her, I had no idea this was happening and it was no wonder John thought they were all CRAZY. She asked if we would like to try again and I told her, "No, we have had quite enough."

So it was that John remained at home the rest of his days. He would swim in the pool for hours on end and really enjoyed it. He really liked it when Tom would come and they could play volleyball and other games in the water. John was getting less and less active around the house and due to a nerve in his leg, which gave him lots of pain, he couldn't sit for any period of time making his days spent either in the pool or in his bed, which was adjustable. Everything in his room worked on remote controls it seemed.

As time passed, John became more dependent on us to move about. Al and I could hardly lift him anymore. He loved to eat, and with little to no exercise, he had gained more weight than he should have. Finally, in April of 2003, Al went on a trip and I was to have John's care to myself. Al wasn't comfortable with leaving like this so he hired an aide to come the three days he was gone, for an hour each day, at the time I had to put John on the toilet and then into the pool. John had been holding his legs stiff so that a person could use their weight and pull him up from his chair, and at the same time pivot him around onto the toilet, and the same thing getting off again. When Al returned from the trip, John stopped helping by stiffening his legs; instead they were like wet noodles.

That meant we had the full weight of John to lift, and it only got worse.

I could see that we needed help badly, so we went to the State office of Developmental Disabilities. We applied for a patient lift for John to help us in our care of him. He already had a lift for the pool, but it was a permanent lift in the concrete.

There were interviews, and interviews. People came to our house and they wrote their reports and always the answer was "NO." It was really getting to us. Finally, they sent a Haitian girl to help us. She was supposed to come for five hours a day, seven days a week. The first thing she said was, "I can't lift him." Then she had a daughter of her own in a nursery and she had to pick her up at 2 P.M. John usually was in the pool until 4 or 5, so she was already gone. She suggested that she help me with other things, like cleaning John's room, making his bed, etc. Do you have any idea how long that takes? Not five hours. I was letting her go home after a couple of hours, as it was very frustrating to have her hanging around. She begged me not to fire her, as she needed the job so badly herself. Saturday came, and I had just about had it. I was ready to scream, so when she was leaving I said to her, "Tomorrow, why don't you stay home with your daughter.

You need to be with her some and I will sign that you were here." I was ready to pay her myself not to come.

You have to understand the system…the Dept. of Developmental Disabilities takes the request for service to Tallahassee, when and if it is O K'd, they turn it over to another company, in our case it was Advocates in Motion, and a lady named Andrea. She, in turn, went to her help supplier, Spectrum Life Care. This last company sends out whatever you really need, like aides or someone to help bathe. They even send material things like pampers or bed protector sheets and cleaning cloths. There is a chain that you have to go through before you receive any service.

Once you get something started, it's hard to turn it off. I might even say you really don't want to turn it off, because you may never get anything again if you turn something down.

I was almost beside myself about this predicament. Here I needed a patient lift, and I got a person who could not lift a patient. On top of that, I got one who pleaded with me to keep her on, even though I know she knew what little help she gave was useless.

She didn't come on Sunday, and it was such a peaceful day for me. I really dreaded the next day, Monday, as I knew it would start all over again. I was on the telephone when the doorbell rang and Al let her in. A few minutes later, I went into the kitchen and Al was alone. I said, "Where is she?"

He said, "You'll never believe this. She was in a car accident over the weekend and she can't work any more. She just came here to get me to sign her work sheet."

I don't know when I have been so relieved. My prayers had truly been answered, albeit, in a most unusual way. God does work in mysterious ways, doesn't he? I know that he knew I just was at my wits end. I told the people at the agency that we didn't need another person to help us. We just needed a patient lift.

Finally, after a couple more people came out to interview us and we were turned down by Tallahassee, Al called the head person at the Department of Developmental Disabilities, and he demanded she send someone who could make an evaluation of our situation so that we could get the patient lift. Now the state had already paid out more to individuals than a lift would have cost them, but that's bureaucracy for you.

On John's last birthday, September 22nd, a wonderful lady, named Connie, who was a registered nurse, came to our house. She had just walked through our front door when she said, "I cannot believe this. Anyone with two eyes can see that you need help."

She also said that nowhere on any application did it mention that either Al or I was a senior citizen. Al was 82 and I was 70, is that senior enough for you?

Connie came on Monday, and on Thursday a patient lift was delivered to our door. It was a gift sent from heaven! She also recommended that John have a companion to visit him several times a week, as she felt he needed interaction with more than just our family members. That is when a beautiful young girl, named Alexandra, started coming three times a week, for three hours a day, to swim with John and just be a friend. She would talk with him for hours, and encourage him to swim laps in the pool. He really looked forward to her coming.

One day Allison, my granddaughter, said, "You know, Mema, I have never seen Uncle John talk so much at a time to one person. He really must like her."

One time when she came, it was storming outside and John couldn't go into the pool, so she was in his room with him and she was helping by dusting the many things that he had sitting around the room. He would tell her about each thing as she took it up to dust. She came to a picture of Susan, with her cats. It had a voice message on it when you pushed a button on the side that said "Merry Christmas, John, from Susan and her cats."

Alexandra said, "John, who is this?"

He said, "Put that down, Sweetheart, don't touch that. That's my other girl friend."

Later Alexander said to me, "I guess he thinks of me as his girl friend, too."

John didn't get much use from all the great things that were coming his way now. The patient lift, which made it so easy for us to move him from one place to another. The wet cloths that were sent to help in cleaning him…only a few months did he enjoy this better life. Only a few months did he get to spend with his friend, Alexandra. Only a few months more did he get to enjoy his pool and swimming.

John with Brian Young, swimming together

John in his pool

19

THE HOLIDAYS

All the holidays were very important to John. He really enjoyed them each one and wanted to do all the traditional things one does. Easter was important to him. When he was small and walking, we would hide the Easter eggs, first in our house, and then if the weather permitted, someone would hide them again in the yard. It was a fun game for him. Even after he was grown he wanted an Easter basket with colored eggs and lots of candy. Each year he got his basket. He pretended to believe in the Easter bunny but I wonder if he actually knew it was us. He used a large basket that I had as a child, and it was always filled with the colorful eggs and lots of the yellow marshmallow chicks, along with jellybeans and miniature candy bars. He loved it and after he became confined to his bed, I would put the basket outside his door and pretend to 'find the basket the bunny left'.

Another festive day for John was the 4th of July. My, how he enjoyed that! Here in Plantation, we always had a parade and there were fire trucks and police sirens and scouts marching and veterans marching and, of course, Mayor Veltri always led the parade. For many years, Al's veterans group, the CBI Veterans, marched in the parade, and John was always so proud to see his dad. One year, Judy was in the parade with the Plantation Junior group and Allison went along with her. We always knew so many in the parade as local scouts and other groups always were included. We would walk from our house to the Plantation City Hall and take chairs to sit under the large shade trees and watch, as that was where the parade ended. Someone always threw candy to the children along the way and John looked forwarded to that. Usually, we had small flags to wave to the marchers as we enjoyed the morning. As a rule, the parade was televised later in the evening and John always wanted to watch again. As he grew older and less able to attend, he would listen from his bed to the sirens and all the drums beating. We would always bring him a souvenir from the parade like candy or a red, white & blue hat or perhaps a small flag. It was a happy day for him, as in the later years, Tom and his kids would come from Raleigh, and we usually had a family picnic or dinner with Judy and her family coming over. It was always a family affair.

Valentine's Day was fun for John also. When he was in school I would get cards for all the class and he would sign his name. We always included a sucker or piece of candy inside the envelope. He would take it to school and then on his return he would show me all the cards he had received from his friends. After he graduated, he didn't receive many cards, but the ones he did receive, he treasured. My brother always sent him one, and then there was Susan. My, how he looked forward to her cards! Susan never missed any occasion to send John a card, even Halloween. There was a group of young people who attended the Methodist Church and they had made it a tradition to visit John on special days. The last Valentines day he had, this group came over and they had each one made him a Valentine. They were all sparkly, and each one had a special note to John. He insisted on keeping them beside him in his bed when he went to sleep that night. The next morning, there was glitter all over the bed where the cards had been. I finally was able to convince him to just hang them on the wall.

Halloween was O K, but he enjoyed it more when he was little, and could dress up and go with the kids from door to door doing trick or treat. Usually, either Al or I would go along to make sure he was O K. One year, he dressed up like a girl, and wore a wig and lipstick. He really made a pretty girl. Several times, when he was older, he wore a shirt to school that had an orange pumpkin painted on the front. He thought this was pretty cool; he was dressed like a pumpkin. He always liked to wear that blonde wig for some reason, too. As he got older, and it was more difficult for him to walk, he didn't take as much interest in this holiday until the last few years. That was when Susan started sending him things to decorate his room for the holiday. She did this for several years, sending paper skeletons, pumpkins, cobwebs, and streamers with different sayings on them, and John did enjoy it when I would decorate his room. Naturally, the grandchildren always came over, and they would go to his room and share their candy. He enjoyed seeing them in their Halloween costumes. Sometimes, even neighbor kids would come in and show off their costumes. Of course John enjoyed the left over candy when it was all over.

His church friends came on most of the holidays, and usually brought him candy or even cupcakes or cookies. On March 17th, 2004, it was St Patrick's Day. John had passed away on March 9th. I was sitting at my computer, trying to make all the horrible thoughts and memories go away, and our doorbell rang. I went to the door, and to my surprise, there was the group from the church. I asked them inside saying "I'm sure you didn't know, but John passed away about a week ago."

One girl spoke up and said, "Yes, we knew. But we had planned to come over and see John today, and since he isn't here, we wanted to come by to see you and bring the cookies that we wanted him to have." She said that they missed John, and he had always been so special to them, and they wanted me to know this. Then each one started telling me what John had meant to them.

One said, "I am in the Junior Olympics swimming, and it has been so hard for me to continue with all the practice I had to do. I had decided to quit, and then I thought about John and how he never quit, and it gave me the courage to keep going, even when I thought I couldn't."

Others agreed that when their schoolwork seemed overwhelming, they remembered John and it prodded them to try harder. They stayed a while and visited and left their cookies, but they left much more…they left me with the knowledge that my John really did count to many people. I wasn't the only one who missed him. A couple of Sundays later, as I was leaving church, one of the girls came to me and put her arms around me and started to cry. Then she said to me, "I miss him, too."

Christmas was always very special to John. Besides the tree with all the decorations and all the gifts, he really enjoyed the carols and the excitement that the little kids showed. We always had Christmas at our house, and then, later, sometimes went to neighbors or to Judy's, but the whole day something was going on. Then, after John and Susan became friends, she would always send him a huge box with all sorts of things inside, each one wrapped individually. She had a friend, who worked at the St. Louis Cardinals ball field, and they were always giving things to the patrons like baseballs with autographs, bobble-head dolls of the players, different banners and pendants, and he would always bring whatever it was to Susan. She would save them up and later send to John. He became quite the Cardinals fan. She would buy him little bears that were dressed like Cardinal ball players, and once sent him a blanket with the Cardinals logo on it. John would take his time and savor each article that she sent. I always said, it really wouldn't make him any difference what she sent to him, he would think it was wonderful. Last Christmas she sent him a little pillow that was shaped like a baseball mitt. It had a removable white baseball in the center. It was really quite cute and A.J. wanted it very badly. He kept hinting to John that he would like to have it, but to no avail. Finally, he just said, "Uncle John, I really want that pillow."

John just smiled and said, "No, it's mine."

Later that evening, I said to John, "Why don't you give that to A.J.? He really likes it."

He said, "Because I am going to give it to him for his birthday." Susan had always said that John could give away anything he wanted to, because it was his to give, and it would make him feel good to be able to give things to people that were his. Anyway, John passed away in March and A.J.'s birthday wasn't until April 15th.

That day I told Al, "I'm going to wrap up that little pillow for A.J. John said he wanted to give it to him for his birthday." So I wrapped it up, and made a card, saying that this was from Uncle John and that he had wanted A.J. to have it. I really think it meant a lot to A.J., because he knew his Uncle John wanted him to have it.

That last Christmas, the friends from the church came by and John was so excited.

Judy and her family were here also. They sang songs to John and talked to him. He kept telling Judy, "Tell them to give me a kiss."

Judy said, "No. John, they aren't here to kiss you, they are here to visit with you and sing Christmas Carols for you."

He got that perturbed look on his face, and he wasn't the least bit happy. Finally he said, "Judy, get me some mistletoe." We all got a laugh out of that. If he had mistletoe, he thought he could surely get a kiss from someone.

That group of young people from United Methodist Church had taken on a mission of working to make money for the Appalachian Service Project. (A.S.P.). Appalachian Service Project's goal was to go into the Appalachian Mountains and rebuild, remodel and repair homes for the less fortunate people, living in this region of our country. The group worked hard all year raising money by having car washes, breakfasts, selling goods, anything that they could do to earn money. They bought materials, tools and supplies for this purpose, and they donated their time for a couple of weeks during the summer, in the Appalachian Mountains. This has been a major endeavor for them. After John passed away, we asked that in lieu of flowers, people donate the money to A.S.P. and to that group of young people, in memory of John. In that way, John could partially repay these young people for making his life a little brighter, and he could help them achieve their goal in their mission of good will, to help the less fortunate and needy families of our country. In his memory and honor, over $2,200.00 was raised, and the kids met their goal of $13,000.00, with 'John's help'. Even after his death, John had made a difference again.

One day that he truly enjoyed, even though it wasn't a holiday, was his own birthday. It really didn't matter about getting gifts, he just enjoyed being made over. He really liked having people come by to see him, and he loved the candles and cake. His last birthday, Tom came from Raleigh, alone, and that really made him happy. John was the center of attention, and he loved that. Even if he was 36 years old, he was just a kid at heart, and he had captured his brother's full attention.

John with his wonderful friend, Susan Brown

Celebrating July 4th, 2003

20

MORE MEMORIES OF JOHN

John had a way with words, possibly not the same way as others, he had his own way. Those people who really knew John, and were around him for any time, would know that when he was pleased with something that you did for him or gave him something that he really liked, he would say, "Purfec" (Perfect) "Purfec." That's the way he would say it.

There were times when he would say, "That's great," or "That's just great." This was when he was really pleased about something that had happened to him or something that he really enjoyed.

If you gave him something that he particularly liked to eat or something that he liked to look at, he might tell you, "My Favorite." You'd say, "How's that John?" and he would answer, "Purfec, My Favorite."

Of course, whenever any female came into his view it was, "Hello, Sweetheart." A lot of people remember being called sweetheart by John. As a general rule he liked everyone, especially women or girls. They were his "Sweetheart." If John didn't like you, he usually had a good reason. He didn't like to be put down, or made fun of, and he didn't like to be teased. You treated him right, and he would like you. That was John.

Another thing he used to say to me, and also to Al, any time he did something that he thought might be the right thing to do, he would say, "Are you proud of me?" He was always asking this question and sometimes about the funniest things, like if he went to the bathroom and he went fast, he would ask if we were proud of him. "Are you proud of me?" He needed us to be proud of everything he did, no matter how menial it was.

In the last few years of John's life, he developed speech impairment. He never did enunciate clearly, but we could always understand him. It was when his tongue was getting thicker and his throat area got larger, that we began to have a problem understanding him. John had a bad habit, when he said something we didn't understand, he would say it again over and over, the same way, so it became a real game with him. He would say something and his Dad would say, "John, I did not quite understand you. What do you want?" John would repeat himself several times until his Dad would ask John to spell it, which he could do very well. Finally, his Dad would understand and ask John if this is what he wanted. John always smiled and said, "Dat's the one!" John and his Dad would always have a laugh after this. Dat's the one!

John had a way of 'playing' people. He knew just what to ask each person, and which of them would turn him down. He used Allison as his 'gofer' when she was around, but he knew that A.J. would probably question anything that John would ask for.

By the same token, he knew his Dad could be talked into almost anything, whereas I would most likely question why he wanted or needed something, and if it was not to his advantage to have that certain thing, I would say "No." No wasn't in Al's vocabulary. John got almost anything he asked for from his dad. We had several birds at this point. Two of them were African Grey parrots, and they had learned many voices of different people. One would use my voice to call the dog or to answer the phone with "Hello." She also would call out to John around 5:30 P.M., "John, get in the sling, get in the sling John."

She would continue until we rolled him through the room, past her cage, to his room. Then she would say, "Hello, John." The other Grey, named Bingo, had taken on John's voice, and he learned to call out, "YO DAD!" That was how John would call his dad when he wanted something special, "YO, Dad." Sometimes the bird would call out, "YO, Dad" and Al would jump up and go to John's room to see what he needed. John would be lying in the bed chuckling to himself and he would say, "That's the bird. That's the bird." It seemed funny to us at the time, but to this day both the birds call out, "John get in the sling" or "Come here, John," and the one that really gets to me is the, "YO, Dad," in John's voice. Bingo seems to do this right at bedtime. I said to Al, "Maybe I should get rid of Bingo if he keeps on with this."

Al said, "No, No, I always want to remember John's voice." So we still have both birds and we still have John's voice.

John loved to swim. They had told us he could not be taught to swim, but he learned from his brother and sister, and from his nephews and niece. His brother would have John go under the water and swim through Tom's legs, as he stood in the shallow water with his legs wide apart. John learned to hold his breath this way, and he also learned to swim under water. He always seemed to prefer swimming under the water from then on.

He had one advantage in having his legs locked at the hips and having a few extra pounds. He could lie on his back and float, and his legs would not sink. He would actually fall asleep, lying on his back, in the deep water, and not sink.

He loved to play volleyball with the kids but he could not hit the beach ball, that's the kind of ball they used, standing up. Instead, he would lie on his back and float until the ball was over his feet. Then he would kick the ball towards his chest, catch it with his hands and then toss it up a little and punch it with his hand. By now, because of the Cerebral Palsy, his fingers were permanently bent, like a fist, and it helped him punch the ball over the net. He never got frustrated, but he would repeat the procedure until he hit it over.

He also insisted that the beach balls were taken out of the pool, so each day when he was told to "Get in the sling" he would swim all around the pool and punch the beach balls out. Sometimes this took a little doing, but he never wanted to get out of the pool until he was satisfied the pool had been cleared of all the balls and that the cover to the pool was straight. In the summer, he didn't have to worry about the pool cover, but in cooler weather, when we wanted to keep the water warm, he worked hard to get that pool cover straight.

He liked to be called "Sheriff John." I think there were several reasons for this. When he was little, he used to have a badge and also a helmet that had a flashing light on top of it. The lady down the street, who lived with her daughter, was always having the paramedics come to her house. Of course the police would come also. John would stand on the corner and direct traffic. Naturally he didn't really direct anyone, they were doing their own thing, but to John, he was directing the traffic. Later he started looking at a television program called Emergency. It was about the lives of paramedics and police and he just loved it. My son, Tom, taped several videotapes of re-runs of Emergency when they were replayed several years later. John would look at these tapes forever, over and over. I think he knew what they were going to say before they said it. One night I was looking at a tape with him and the commercial came on. It was advertising something that you couldn't buy anymore. I said, "John, let mom show you how to fast forward the commercials so you don't have to look at them."

"No, No. That's alright," he said, "I like to look at them." I tried to talk him into doing the fast forward thing to no avail. He just wanted to see the whole thing. Another reason he liked to be called "Sheriff John" was because one of his favorite people was the Broward County Sheriff, Nick Navarro. He thought Sheriff Nick was something very special. Anytime he would be on television, John always wanted to hear what he had to say.

John spent many hours daily swimming in our pool. We heated the water on colder days and he never seemed to mind the temperature. The water was his equalizer. In the pool, he could walk and move about, something that he could not do on ground. We would always turn on the radio to a station with music, and John would dance in the pool as he listened. This was his entertainment and the way he spent a good part of his day, especially in the last few years. There are steps leading down into the pool and John would sit on these steps, swaying back and forth to the music, with a smile on his face. This was his enjoyment. One time he told his friend, Alexandra, that the steps were his stage. "That's where I dance," he said.

John loved to swim and he was in his glory when others would be in the pool with him. Tom usually came down several times a year and he would bring his two kids, Tommy and Ashley, and they would play in the pool with John. Volleyball was one of the favorite games and John was actually pretty good at it. Another game they played was sort of a tag game. John would 'chase' the kids around the pool and they would squeal "kisser whale, kisser whale." Then, when he caught them, they would get one of his kisses. He was pretty fast in the water and he sort of moved around like a small whale.

As I said before, John enjoyed watching his television. Everything worked on remote, so he had a C.D. player for listening to his C.D's, he had a VCR, a DVD and of course, his very favorite, the television. His radio was behind his head on a shelf built into the bed headboard. This shelf also contained an intercom so that he could reach us if he needed something in the night. It was wireless and worked like a doorbell, you just had to push a button and a bell would ring in our bedroom. Many of his treasures could be found there, his wallet, pictures that he loved to look at, notes from Susan, his M & M dispenser, and all the things he loved. Tom had decorated John's room before he got married and left home. They had shared this room at one point in time, and Tom had every wall covered with posters of the things John loved. The Beatles, The Monkees, Bruce Springsteen, Star Wars, anything that John liked. There were no walls showing, just posters. They are still there. The only thing we removed was a Cardinals towel and a picture of a little angel with a poem that read: "Turn not your head or hide me in the dark, etc." That picture will remain with John in his grave through eternity. John's room was different. John was different. Sometimes it's very nice to be different. Try looking at things with a different perspective. Look at them through John's eyes. You might be very pleasantly surprised.

Then there were the trips we took together. Many of them were CBI Veteran's occasions, like National Board Meetings or State Reunions. The CBI Vets were WWII Veterans who served America and the world in China, Burma and India. Al had been a pilot stationed there, and he flew a C-47, which supplied food and supplies to our armed forces on the ground in China, Burma and India. The main enemy was the weather, since flying over the Himalaya Mountains during monsoon weather was treacherous. The enemy on the ground was the Japanese. These veterans had formed a real bond and all these many years after the end of the war, they still got together to enjoy the company of friends who served in the war with them. John went with us to all of the get-togethers. Several of our

CBI friends took their children when they were little. All the kids got to know each other, and they looked forward to the next event. One young boy was Patrick DeLong, the son of our very dear friends in Miami. There was Brenda Knox, the daughter of Ted and Irene in Boca, there was Emily Ann Diana, the daughter of Emily and Manny Diana, and there was John. The four kids really enjoyed their times together. At one of the reunions, I had left John in his wheelchair by the poolside. He was very capable of handling himself in the pool, much more there than out of the pool. John decided he wanted to dive in and he had his suit on. He rolled his wheel chair over to the side and leaned over and dove into the pool. By all accounts, from those who were watching, two ladies from another group jumped into the pool immediately, trying to 'rescue' John, while all the CBI people there were calling, "It's O K, he knows how to swim." The other kids really thought this was very funny.

We traveled to Ft. Walton Beach, to Ft. Myers and to Orlando several times. Orlando was where they usually had their Christmas party. There was always a Puja Parade and John liked to lead the parade. Everyone dressed in different attire, some as soldiers, others as Chinese or whatever he or she thought appropriate. The members of this organization made it a point to always include John in everything. One time, the National Commander at the time made John an honorary member. John thought this was really great.

Once, when they had a National Reunion in Orlando, it took place in the 'Twin Towers', which was the same hotel with two towers and many floors in each tower. They shared the same lobby and ground floor rooms. We had just arrived in one of the meeting rooms on the ground floor and were visiting with friends. I looked around and couldn't find John. I started asking first one person and then another, "Have you seen a little boy in a wheelchair?" They started pointing me in the direction John had taken, through double doors and into the lobby.

"Why yes," said one lady, "I opened the door for him."

There I was in the lobby, confused about the elevators, one leading to one tower, the other to the second tower. I wondered if John remembered which set of elevators to take. I thought I will go to the room first, and then we need to put out an all points bulletin for him. I took the elevator to the floor our room was on, the doors opened, and there was John, in front of the door to our room. He remembered the right floor and room number. He never forgot a thing. His mind was a steel trap.

One year the CBI National reunion was held in Las Vegas. John was a little older then, and so we took Tom with us to stay with John when we were in meetings where he wouldn't want to be. He was always welcomed, but as he was getting older, and he wasn't as interested in being around all us old folks all the time. I certainly didn't want another incident like the one that had happened in Orlando, where he took off and went back to the room to watch television or something. So Tom went with us. John wasn't 21 yet, and he wasn't allowed in the casinos where betting was taking place. We had rented a car there, and one day Tom put John in the car, and they went to a casino called Circus, Circus. There they had games that children could play. You didn't win money, you won prizes. There was a game where you threw bags filled with sand and tried to make a 'Tic, Tac, Toe'. It wasn't that easy either. You had to throw three little bags and make them land in a row, either up and down or across, or from one corner to the other. Tom let John play, and twice he made the Tic, Tac, Toe, so he brought home two little dolls that looked like Peanuts, the comic strip character. They now sit on a shelf in John's room. He did it all by himself and he was so very proud. I later tried to do it, and I couldn't make it.

That same trip, we took a side venture to meet a cousin of mine that I had never met before. He and his wife and daughter live in Simi Valley California, a little north of Los Angeles. I knew his mother and father both, but he had never been back to the central part of the country, so none of our family had ever met him. John took a liking to his cousins immediately. We had dinner with them and spent the evening getting to know each other. The next day I looked up an old girl friend of mine who had moved to Los Angeles when she and I were in the 8th grade. I had kept in touch via Christmas Cards but had not seen her in all those years. This was one of our happiest trips that we would take together.

Being a child of routine, everything John did had to be done just one way, the way he wanted. Our swimming pool was heated during the cooler months and after swimming, John's dad would replace a blue plastic bubbled blanket to cover the water. It was rolled up into two pieces and had to be unrolled, which was a difficult task outside of the pool, so John's dad did the best he could. It was never satisfactory for John, who was still in the pool, and John's dad would say, "John, Get in the sling." The sling was the lift that we used to get John out of the pool. This was a regular occurrence because John was not interested in getting in the sling until he had removed all the folds and wrinkles from the pool cover. He would work his way around the cover, even in the deep water, until he was satisfied that the pool cover was in place. It took John some time but he was determined not to quit until he was done. The most ironic thing was the fact that one of our African Grey parrots, Angel, learned the phrase, "Get in the sling, John," and sad to say, after John left us, Angel would continue to say "Get in the sling, John." It is very heart breaking.

Over the years, and especially the past ten years, I became quite interested in birds, sort of a hobby and something I could do at home while I was with John. He didn't need my attention often, but when he did, I needed to be close. The birds became a big part of my life and also John's life. He had a glass front aviary in his room which he really enjoyed watching. It had lights that were on a timer and would go off in the evening and on in the morning. The aviary contained many beautiful finches of all colors, Cordon Bleus, Gouldians, Societies, Orange Cheeks and several others including one male canary, who sang beautifully. The finches had babies and raised them in this aviary, feeding them, etc. and were of great interest to John. He could lie in his bed and watch for hours.

We had a large aviary on our screened patio that contained about 50 finches. We also had quite a few cages that Al attached to the wall, and those were used for breeding and for quarantine purposes, when it was necessary. Someone suggested that I let a couple of birds loose on the patio, to fly freely, and John could watch them better while he was swimming in the pool. So we decided to do so. At first, I let a couple of Weavers out and they were really pretty to watch. I put an artificial tree in the corner of the patio, next to the pool, so they would have a place to perch. This went good for a little while until the Weavers started weaving the doors to the little cages shut using miscellaneous materials they found, like grass or pieces of string. It was their nature to weave, and weave they did. They started tearing up anything that could be used as string, and they would weave the doors so that they could not be opened. Each morning, when I would go to feed the birds in the cages, I had to take a knife or scissors to get the doors open. John thought this was very funny. He was upset when I told him I would have to put the Weavers back in the enclosed aviary, since they were causing trouble for me in caring for the other birds. I decided to try another type of finch, so he could enjoy them, and I chose a pair of Zebra finches. This pleased John and the Weavers were contained so they couldn't do any damage to the birdcages on the patio. The little Zebras were happy as they flew back and forth, and their wing strength became stronger, so they were hard to catch. Since they weren't causing any havoc, we decided to let them fly free, at least on the patio area. Then spring came, and with spring came the need to procreate. While Zebra finches do breed nearly all year round, the need to do so becomes greater it seems, in the spring of the year. So they started looking for a place to build a nest and decided on the artificial tree at the corner of our patio, next to the pool. It never occurred to me to make them change their plans, so in a few weeks they had eggs. After two weeks of incubation, three of the five eggs hatched. Then about two weeks later, one day John was swimming in the pool and he started calling, "Mom! Mom! Take a look! Take a look!" I went outside to see what the problem was, and there, on a raft that was floating in the pool, lay three nearly dead, very wet little Zebra finch babies, and a mother and father finch swooping back and forth over the float, making all kinds of noise. It seems the little birds had tried to fledge from their nest, and not having enough strength in their new little wings, they plunged into the pool. John was watching all this, and he maneuvered himself to their rescue, scooped them up in his hands, and carefully placed them on the floating raft, then he called for my help, "Mom! Mom! Take a look! Take a look!" I carefully placed the three little birds back into their nest, and placed the nest inside one of the small cages hanging on the wall.

Then I had to catch the mother and father bird and put them into the small cage with their babies. John laughed, as I ran back and forth, from one side of the pool to the other, trying to catch the now, very strong mother and father birds. All of the babies lived and John was so proud that he had saved their lives. That was the last time we let birds fly loose on our patio.

I joined a bird society and at one time was President. I attended many national and local shows and our organization had a show of their own every year. In August 2003, we were trying to drum up interest in the community for our show and one of our members got the Miami Herald newspaper to write an article on the up coming show and our birds. A lady by the name of Georgia Tasker came out and did interviews with Ruth, the president, and me, and the subject of how we became interested in birds came up. I told her a little about John and that must have peaked her interest. She sent her photographer to our house and he took lots of pictures of all the birds, including John looking at his glass front aviary.

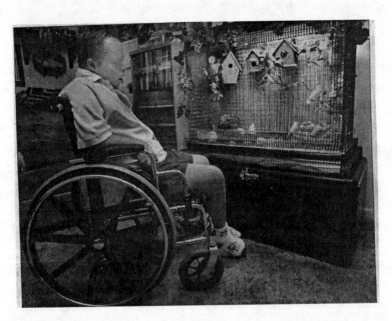

When the article came out, there were two pages with pictures of our birds, including the one of John looking at his aviary, and a good deal of the article was about John. I was a little embarrassed, as I had wanted it to be an article on our club, not one about John. Everyone said, it's a good human-interest story and will probably attract a lot of attention for the club. I think they were being generous, but it was a done deal and nothing I could do to retract it. John was always so proud that his picture had been in the paper. Later, when John passed away, we had his obituary notice in the Fort Lauderdale Sun Sentinel newspaper. The same lady, Georgia Tasker, noticed the obituary in the rival newspaper and said to her reporter, "This is the same young man we did an article about last August. Get me a story on him for our paper." They contacted me and asked all about what had happened to John, and to our surprise, she wrote an article, including a picture of John looking at his aviary in the Miami Herald, and it was two columns long. John would have been so very proud. The article in the Sun Sentinel was about an inch high and had cost us $200. The free article written by Georgia Tasker from the Miami Herald was two columns long, with a picture, and it cost nothing. That article attracted attention of many people, and one lady sent a donation to one of the charities we had named, Hospice, because she had read the article and was impressed since she had a daughter with Down Syndrome. John…still doing good!!

As I look back over the years, there were many times we had together that are very pleasant memories, so many that I had nearly forgotten some of them. Everyone has gotten older now, but I remember them as they were then. That's how I like to remember John, with a smile that would light up a room or your heart, and a way of looking at things that no one else quite understood. He saw beauty in the ugly; he heard music when there was none. What a gift he had, looking through those rose colored glasses. Looking through eyes that filtered out the imperfections of the world. He was truly Up Syndrome.

Niece, Ashley and John

Sharing time with brother Tom,
Sister Judy, Niece Ally and Nephew, A.J.

21

MARCH 9, 2004

That's what it says on his death certificate, but I don't know if that is entirely accurate. That was a Tuesday morning, very early, 12:55 A.M. it reads, respiratory failure.

My, how our lives are controlled with certificates. We get one when we are born, we get one when we die, and for many people, they get quite a few more during their lives. John got several certificates during his life. He got five for being the best child of the week in school. He got one for being the 'Best of the Class', and was on television for this one during his senior year. My brother even sent him one that said "Super Nephew Award", and it still hangs on his bedroom door. Then he got a certificate saying he had graduated from High School. Yes, even John had many certificates in his short life.

His death certificate says March 9th, 2004, but it really all started on the Sunday before, March 7th. John had lunch while he was swimming in the pool, something that he did nearly every day. That day I made him pizza, which he normally loved. I went onto the porch and found him stuffing the pizza into the chlorine dispenser. I told him to stop, but he continued doing it. Al came out and he told him to stop and took the dispenser away from him. This was a little strange behavior for John but I really didn't think about it until later. Around 5 P.M., he wanted to get out of the pool, another thing that was a little unusual, as he never wanted to get out before, but I thought he was probably tired, actually I didn't give it much thought at all. As Al was pumping the patient lift that was lifting him out of the pool, John asked if he could have Kentucky Fried Chicken strips for dinner. After getting John into bed, Al went to Kentucky Fried Chicken and got that for him for his dinner. We were having something that he couldn't eat too well, so that worked out O K. Many times Al would go and get John something different to eat. He was like that, a good Dad, and John loved to eat. It was one of the things that he really enjoyed. He liked Subway and Taco Bell and Kentucky Fried Chicken. Fortunately, they were all in close distance to our house.

John started eating and then pushed his dinner aside saying he couldn't eat it. Al was upset with him and he told John that was the last time he was ever going to get him something special. Of course, he didn't really mean it, but those words would come back to haunt us later. As the night wore on, John was calling us for one thing or another. I had fed him a little fruit for dinner, a thing that I never did much as feeding himself was one of the few things John could do. I had made an exception this night. He also wanted chocolate milk and I gave that to him. Still, he kept calling for one thing and then the other, the urinal, some water, on and on. Finally Al said, "I can't go for him any more. I have to get up early tomorrow to go to the doctor. Can you get him next time?"

I said, "Sure," and I went into his room and got on the bed beside John. We watched some of the Emergency tape he had. He loved that show and my son Tom had made several tapes of re-runs of that program. I could hear he was getting a little choked up it seemed. Next, he asked me for some Orange Sherbet. I told him "No, you will have to wait until tomorrow. It's 11:30. We need to get some sleep." (It was Orange Sherbet, for heavens sake. Why couldn't I get up and get him a little Orange Sherbet? What did it matter if it was 11:30 at night? Really, what did it matter? I ask myself this question nearly every day. That Orange Sherbet will haunt me until my dying day. Now that I look back, maybe that Orange Sherbet might have soothed his throat. Oh, if I could only go back and give him a little Orange Sherbet!) Then he kept saying he wanted something, "NOW."

I said, "John I understand you want something now, but what is it you want now?" His speech had become slurred the past few years and when he couldn't make himself understood he would spell the words. Then he spelled P-A-R-E-N-T-S.

I said, "You want parents?"

"Yes, yes." he said.

I said "John, I'm your mother, I am a parent."

Then he said, "Dad, too." I called Al, to see if he was sleeping already. He came in and we agreed that we needed to call the doctor, because the antibiotics John was taking for his sinus infection just didn't seem to be working. Naturally, the doctor couldn't be reached.

We talked for a few minutes and finally I said, "You know, forget the doctor, call 911. He needs some oxygen I think," and Al went into the kitchen, to phone 911 for emergency help. I was standing by John talking to him while Al made the phone call. About half way through the call, John looked up at me, closed his eyes and he stopped breathing. I screamed to Al to hurry, and I started blowing into John's mouth, and continued to do so until the Paramedics arrived, which was only a couple of minutes. They had actually been on the way during the phone call. They rushed in and told us to get out. There were about five of them, I'm not sure now. I was so scared and I didn't know what to do. We had called them a little before midnight. I sat in the kitchen while they worked on John. They were there about 45 minutes.

Then the lady came in and said they were going. I thought that they were going back to wherever they came from and I said, "Well, what should I do for John now?"

She said, "We'll be taking him to the hospital. You can follow us." Then I saw them rolling John out through the family room, down the hall, and out the front door, to their waiting ambulance. I quickly called Judy, and then Al and I followed them to the hospital. Even then, I had no idea of how this was going to end.

From then on, the concept of time left me, and even now I can't remember exactly what happened when. I remember our minister came to the hospital. It was about 2:30 or 3 A.M. I later learned that my daughter had called him. I remember wondering how he knew we were there. He kept talking to me, also the doctor talked with me some, and then another doctor came, and then they said I needed to make a decision. I thought they meant that we had to decide whether to leave John in the hospital, or take him home that night or morning rather. They said, no, that wasn't what they were talking about. It seems he had been put on a temporary respirator, and now he had to either be taken off altogether, or have a tracheotomy operation to put in a permanent respirator. They said he probably wouldn't live through the operation, and that he had brain damage, because his heart had stopped on the way to the hospital, and they didn't know how bad it was. I kept thinking, of course he has brain damage, he has Down Syndrome. I couldn't make the decision to remove the respirator. I told Dr. Foster, "I can't tell you to kill my son, I just can't do that."

He said, "Then I will make the decision for you. He is my patient, and I took an oath to do what was best for my patients, and I think it is best to let John go."

My minister told me I had to let him go. He said, "You don't want him to live like this. Hasn't he had enough?" Dr. Foster said John could never go home again, and would have to go into a nursing home, if he made it through the operation. It was very doubtful that he would ever open his eyes again. In the early morning, they sent me home to wait for my son, Tom, to arrive from Raleigh. Judy had called him the night before and he was flying in on the first available flight. When I got home I couldn't sleep, and I needed to talk with someone, so I called my friend in Alabama, Ginny. She had known John since he was six years old. She knew how much he meant to me. I just had to talk with someone who might understand.

I was waiting for Tom to come, and the doorbell rang. I went to the door and there stood Steve, a very good friend from our bird club. Steve and I had been through many good and bad times together. He was a very dear friend. He said Ginny had e-mailed him about John and he had to come. He was at work in South Miami when he read the e-mail.

He went to his boss and said, "I have a good friend who is in trouble and I am taking a sick day." He got into his car and drove up to Plantation, and there he was. He told me I needed to be with John and that he was going to drive me to the hospital. He would come back to my house and wait until my son came, then bring him to the hospital. So that's what we did. Steve drove me to the hospital. John was still in the emergency room and Al, my daughter, and her husband were also there. John was still the same. Still hadn't opened his eyes, and still on the temporary respirator. Dr. Foster knew how I felt about not giving up. He said he would go to work, and after his hours were over, he would return and then take John off the respirator if there had still been no improvement. Before Steve could leave, Tom came in. He had rented a car and drove straight to the hospital. We remained there all day and in the late afternoon everyone insisted that I go home. Steve left with us, and Al and I went home. Judy, Tom and John Stoner stayed and waited for the doctor.

Hospice had been called, and after Dr. Foster removed the respirator, about 6 P.M., John continued to breathe on his own. No one expected this. They moved him from the emergency room to a hospice room in the hospital. About 10:00 P.M., Tom walked home from the hospital as he was very tired, and it looked like this was going to be a long wait. That was our Monday.

About 1:30 A.M., on Tuesday morning March 9th, 2004, Judy and John Stoner came to our house. I wasn't asleep yet but Al had fallen asleep. They told us that John had passed away just a few minutes ago. Actually according to the 'certificate' the exact time was 12:55 A.M.

The following day was spent making arrangements to have a service. I just could not have a funeral. By all accounts, it looked like there was going to be quite a few people who would be coming. Judy's minister, Pastor Tim, agreed to a combination service of himself and our Minister, Pastor Volz. He also offered his church, as our Lutheran church was where Judy had been married and I just couldn't stand having it there. Also, the Methodist church was much larger and they had a fellowship hall that we could use for 'visitation' prior to the service. I did not want a "viewing". It was to be a closed casket. We decided that this would not be a funeral. It would be a celebration of John's life.

Judy and Allison took things belonging to John and pictures of him during his short life, and they made a tribute to him for people to see in the Fellowship Hall. Ladies of that church made all sorts of sandwiches and snacks and punch to serve those who came to see us. We had the visitation from 11:00 A.M. until 1:00 P.M. John's favorite music was played in the background at the fellowship hall. The Beatles and the Monkees were heard for the last time. Since we didn't want to have this on Hibby's birthday, which was March 12th, we waited until Saturday, March 13th to pay tribute to our son. Tom's wife, Susan, and two children, Ashley and Tommy, flew down from Raleigh on Friday.

The casket was closed with beautiful flowers on top. John's picture was projected on the overhead screens, which usually are used to project bible scriptures during the sermons. Both the ministers gave talks about John and about his life. A.J. went up and read the Prayer of St. Frances, with his sister and his two cousins by his side.

Then, Tom went up and he gave a little talk saying:

"I would like to thank everyone for coming today, and I want to thank those of you who were able to share some of your lives with John. I cannot tell you how much that meant to him, and to my Mother and Father.

A couple of my brother's hero's, whose names were also John, passed away at an early age as well. John Lennon and John Kennedy. They both died without fulfilling their potential. This was not the case with my brother, John, as he got everything, and more, out of the body that he was given. Because of that, he is my hero.

John was not my handicapped brother. John was not my Down Syndrome brother. John was my brother, and he was my best friend.

John, I know that you are now in a better place, but words cannot describe how much I am going to miss you."

After that, Judy went up and she told about how John always seemed to make us laugh. She told several funny stories about John. Before she started telling the stories she said:

"Through all the sadness, grief and hurt that has come from this past week, there have also been moments where we remembered who John REALLY was, and those moments made us smile. I'd like to share a few of those stories with you so you could also know who he was. See, God made him physically handicapped, but he gifted him with an extraordinary way of looking at life. He had a smile that would light a room and he had a rather witty sense of humor, seasoned with his version of reality.

(First story) The Doctor Foster story…When the doctor was a little late for an appointment that John had with him, he came in saying, "Well,

John, how are you today?" John replied, "Well, It's about time!" Then, trying to make him co-operate with the doctor my mother said, "John, this is a good man. Don't you remember, he was your grandmother's doctor and took care of her, remember?"

To this John replied, "Well, no wonder she's dead!"

(Second story) His favorite group of musicians was the Monkees. He always wanted to celebrate Mickey Dolenz' birthday. When he went on a field trip with his school to Washington, D.C., he reprimanded the bus driver for not going by Peter Tork's house.

(Third story) She told the story about the "big pants," where when he kept calling a friend of his father's fat and was told not to say that, John said, "Hey, did you know you have really big pants?"

(Forth story was the napkin story where he took real napkins as souvenirs home with him).

"These are the memories I want to keep of my brother, the ones that make me smile."

After the service, we accompanied John to his final resting place.

John was laid to rest at Lauderdale Memorial Gardens, in the Veteran's section. It was a private burial, just our family members, and Steve with his daughter, Shannon, and my friend Noreene, all very dear friends.

Judy had everyone over to her house after the services and all the food that had been sent to us was put out and I cannot tell you how many people came. Much of the rest of the week was a blur to me, and until I looked at the notes and the 'sign-in' book which was at the visitation, I really don't remember but a very few people who attended. For weeks afterwards different people would say something about the services and I didn't remember them being there. It wasn't that I didn't care, it was just all like a horrible nightmare, one from which I wouldn't wake up. People have told me that John is so much better off now. He isn't in pain, and he is out of his crippled body. I know in my head that they are right, but my heart, oh, in my heart, I do miss him so and I just want to scream at them, "I know he is better off now, but I am not, and I doubt I ever will be!"

22

GRIEF COUNSELING

I took part in a grief-counseling program at the United Methodist Church a few weeks after John's passing. Judy, my daughter, and I went together, once a week, for several weeks. Everyone there had lost a loved one but I was surprised that several had lost their children. They were having the same problems with accepting their loss as I was. As one of our healing processes, we were asked to write a letter to our loved ones telling them our feelings. Here is what I wrote:

June 7th, 2004

My dearest John,

Today I am supposed to write you a letter as part of a Grief program your sister and I have attended since you left us. What can I say? I miss you so very much, my heart is bleeding almost with my grief. Every day I cry when I think of you and sometimes it is hard for me to stop. All sorts of things have happened since you left. I had a tooth fall out, I had my foot operated on and I had a violent reaction to something and had to take medicine for two weeks to cure that. Things around the house are breaking all the time. It's like nothing is going right, not since you left us.

I want so badly to hold you in my arms and tell you how very much I love you. I never took the time when you were here to do so many things. I have so many regrets I cannot tell you all the things I wish I had said to you or done for you. I just wish I had tried harder to make your life more pleasant for you. You never asked for much, and you got so very little. If I could, I would do things much differently. I hope somewhere in your heart that you can forgive me for failing you in so many ways.

John, I know that if there truly is a place called heaven that you are there. I want to believe that so very much. My faith is weak, not like Judy's, and I have so many doubts but I truly wish with all my heart that she is right. If so, I know that Papa and Mom-mom and others are with you now and that you are happy for once and for all.

When you were a little boy I wrote a poem in the form of a letter to you in the hope that when I died, you would read it. Little did I know that you would go before me! So I am going to include that letter/poem in this letter to you now.

"A Letter to my Son"

My dearest son,

How does a mother tell her child how much he's filled her wants,
Or of the precious moments that are treasured in her thoughts?
Each day you've brought me happiness. Each hour you bring me love.
Your smiles and laughter are my joy sent from the Lord above.
Some say you are retarded…That you cannot understand.
But your life could be a pattern for every living man.
You see beauty in the ugly. You hear music when there's none.
And there's no way of counting the many hearts you've won.
Though you may never know it, you've made my life complete.
You give me hope and courage, when I may feel defeat.
You've made me happy when I'm sad and shown me there is hope.
At things which used to trouble me, you've shown me how to cope.
And so, dear John, I thank you for being as you are.
A life line to hang on to—my shining, guiding star.

December 1973

And so you were, my life line to hang on to and now that you are gone I don't know how to cope with my life.

I don't know how to end this letter to you. You will never read it. I love you dearly and I miss you more each day. Today your dad and I went to a store and I found a wind chime with birds on it. We will bring it out to the cemetery soon. I also got a windmill thing that Judy said you really loved and we will put that in with your flowers.

Please, if you know my feelings, show me some sign. Am I just blowing in the wind? Are you aware of the emptiness you have left with us? I will close this letter to you now hoping that in some way you will know what I have written.

Love from me always, Mom

THIS LETTER, ALONG WITH OTHER LETTERS FROM PEOPLE IN MY GRIEF GROUP TO THEIR LOVED ONES, WAS BURNED DURING A CEREMONY AT UNITED METHODIST CHURCH IN PLANTATION, FLORIDA, AND THE ASHES WERE BLOWN AMONG THE FLOWERS IN THE CHURCH YARD.

While attending one of the grief counseling meetings, called "Walking the Mourner's Path," we read a short story about a ship. It went something like this:

"I was standing on the shore watching the beautiful ship as she spread her white sails in the morning breeze, and starts her journey across the ocean blue. She is an object of beauty and strength, and I stood and watched her until, at length, she is but a speck of white cloud just where the sea and sky come down to meet each other.

Then someone at my side said, "Now she is gone, and we will never see her here again." But gone where? It occurred to me, she is only gone from my mind and sight, that is all. She is still the same wonderful ship that left our shores with sails held strong against the winds. Her diminished size is in me, not in her, and just at the moment that someone says, "There, she is gone" on that distant shore, beyond our sight, others watch and wait and take up the glad shout, "HERE SHE COMES, AT LAST."

And such is dying…we say goodbye on this side of the water but from the other side rings out the shouts of others, "Hello, we have been waiting for you."

I pray this is the way it will be…but no one really knows. My one hope is that one day I will be able to see my son again. One day, I can relive a yesterday. I can hold him in my arms and say I love you. I can take his face in my hands and tell him how proud I am of him. But if tomorrow never comes, I still have the memories of my precious son.

Bench by grave

23

THE MUSIC HE LOVED

John loved music and after he passed I listened, probably for the first time, to the words of some of the songs he loved to hear. His favorite groups were the Monkees and the Beatles. A couple of their songs that he liked in particular were: <u>Yesterday</u>, <u>Love</u>, <u>Love, Love</u>, <u>I want to be Free</u> and <u>Let It Be</u>. He would listen for hours, and when I really heard the words, it became apparent to me why he loved them. They said a lot about him....

"Yesterday, all my troubles seemed so far away,
Now it looks as though they're here to stay,
Oh, I believe in yesterday.
Suddenly, I'm not half the man I used to be,
There's a shadow hanging over me.
Oh, yesterday came suddenly.
Why, he had to go. I don't know,
He wouldn't say. I said something wrong.
Now I long for yesterday.
Yesterday, love was such an easy game to play,
Now I need a place to hide away.
Oh, I believe in yesterday."

Wouldn't it be wonderful if we could have yesterday back, for just a short time? So many things we could change or do differently. Yes, yesterday all my troubles seemed so far away and it looks like now they're here to stay. There is a shadow hanging over me, and I would like to know why he had to go, so suddenly. I do long for yesterday and all the good times we had, but they are gone and cannot return, that was yesterday.

"Love, Love, Love
Love, Love, Love
All you need is Love, Love,
Love is all you need."

John was the living proof that "Love is all you need." He gave so much love to all he met, whether they were family or friends. He truly believed that Love is all you need.

"I want to be free,
Like the blue birds flying by me,
Like the waves out on the blue sea,
If your love has to tie me,
Don't try me, say goodbye to me.
I want to be free."

And so he is now free, like the blue birds flying by me, and the waves out on the blue sea. My love cannot tie him here any longer, but the very hardest part now is to say goodbye to him. I prefer not to say goodbye, but until we meet again, dear John.
Never Say Good-bye.

And finally the one that makes the most sense is this one:

"When I find myself in times of trouble,
Mother Mary comes to me,
Speaking words of wisdom, Let it be.
And in my hour of darkness, she is standing right in front of me,
Speaking words of wisdom,
Let it be, let it be, let it be,
Whispering words of wisdom, let it be.
When the broken hearted people living in the world of greed,
There will be an answer, Let it be.
For though they may be parted, there's still a chance that they will see,

And there will be an answer, Let it be.
Let it be, let it be, let it be.
There will be an answer. Let it be, let it be.
Whisper words of wisdom, Let it be."

And now I will have to "Let it be." Those are whispered words of wisdom, and I know there is an answer to what has happened in my hour of darkness, and I will truly try to "Let it be!"

It is said, "When your parents die, you are an Orphan.
When your spouse dies, you are a widow or widower.
But when your child dies......

THERE ARE NO WORDS FOR THAT!"

MARCH 9, 2004...the other end of the **DASH.**

John's final resting place in foreground,
Veteran's Memorial in background.

Looking back over the years since that fateful September day in 1967, I ask myself, "Was it worth it?" If I could go back in time and if I had a choice of either having John in my life or not, would I do it again?

I try to imagine what my life would have been without John. What would my family have been like had he not been born?

While there was hurt and anguish caused by his untimely birth and by his sudden death, I know that my other children, my husband and I are all better people for having had John in our lives.

Knowing what I know now, was it worth it? Would I do it again? The answer to that question is, "<u>Oh, yes! In a heartbeat.</u>" What a wondrous journey it has been walking hand-in-hand down life's path with my "Up Syndrome" son, John. It has truly been a glorious experience I would never give up!

EPILOGUE

My son, Hibby, along with others, has asked me why I wanted to write this book. There isn't any one answer, perhaps there should be and then it might make more sense. I can't say I wrote it for this reason or that reason. I wrote it for several reasons.

When I think back, I guess I actually started writing this book 36 years ago when I started writing the journal about John and his progress, right after he was born. At that time, I wanted to put down everything he did and when he did it in hopes that some other mother who had a Down Syndrome child might find something of interest in it, or find some comfort in reading it. Perhaps just knowing a little about someone who had walked that road might be encouragement to others. I suppose, in a way, that is still my goal and if you are walking this path I have taken I hope you will appreciate the precious life of the child you were given, and each day, let them know how very much they are wanted and they are loved.

This is not my only goal for writing about John and his life. It isn't just about John, though he obviously is the main person involved. It is the story of how his life, as meaningless as it may have seemed to some people, his existence on this earth, made a difference to so many people. How he, in so many small, yet very meaningful ways, touched different people and possibly changed their lives. First, there was his family, then his relatives, but even more importantly, there were people we had no idea had received something from just knowing John, if even for a short period of time.

Secondly, I started writing about my son right after we laid him to rest. It was a way I could put into words things I could not say aloud. It was a way of letting go. Therapy, perhaps, but I needed to wring this from my body, so I wrote. I cried and I wrote, and that was another reason for this book.

Finally, if you have gotten this far, reading all my thoughts, looking into my soul, it must have held your interest to some degree. If you only

learn one thing from this writing, that life is so very short and so very frag-
ile, and each life must be cherished every day, then this is worth the writing, and perhaps, worth the reading. May I please leave you with these
thoughts…Eat your ORANGE SHERBET today! Savor its flavor! Enjoy
it to the fullest, because tomorrow may never come….
and…. **NEVER SAY GOOD-BYE**.

Souvenir glass from John's Prom

ABOUT THE AUTHOR

Melba Jo (Heim) Wilkat was born and raised in Little Rock, Arkansas. She graduated from Little Rock Senior High School in 1951 and continued her formal education for three years at Arkansas State Teachers College in Conway, Arkansas. She married and moved first to St. Louis, Missouri, for sixteen years where her children were born. Later the family moved to Plantation, Florida, after her husband was job transferred.

She is the wife of her husband Albert, a professional engineer, the mother of four children and grandmother of four grandchildren. Her life after her last child, John, was born was that of a mother concerned with the welfare of her son, born with Down Syndrome and Cerebral Palsy. Much of her time was devoted to helping him lead a full life as if he were a normal child, and in making a better place for other children with special needs.

Her knowledge of people with disabilities was obtained from associations with Professionals and other parents with disabled children, coupled with her own first hand experience of living with and caring for a disabled child.

After the death of her beloved son, she decided to write a book in hopes of helping others with similar problems, also as a therapy in coping with her own grief, and finally, understanding the problems of living life after the loss of a child who had been such a tremendous part of her family and her own life.

0-595-34228-0

LaVergne, TN USA
19 December 2010
209366LV00007B/36/A